O9-BUB-972

AN EXPENSIVE WAY TO MAKE BAD PEOPLE WORSE

*An Essay on Prison Reform
from an Insider's Perspective*

JENS SOERING

Lantern Books • New York
A Division of Booklight Inc

2004
Lantern Books
One Union Square West, Suite 201
New York, NY 10003
Copyright Jens Soering, 2004

All rights reserved. No part of this book may be reproduced, stored in a
retrieval system or transmitted in any form or by any means, electronic,
mechanical, photocopying, recording or otherwise, without the written
permission of Lantern Books.

Printed in Canada

Library of Congress Cataloging-in-Publication Data

Soering, Jens.
An expensive way to make bad people worse : an essay on prison reform
from an insider's perspective / by Jens Soering.
p. cm.
Includes bibliographical references.
ISBN 1–59056–076–0
1. Prisons—United States. 2. Corrections—United States. I. Title.
HV9471.S4 2004
365.'7'0973—dc22
2004009073

NEW LEAF PAPER

ENVIRONMENTAL BENEFITS STATEMENT

An Expensive Way to Make Bad People Worse is printed on New Leaf Reincarnation Matte,
made with 100% recycled fiber, 50% post-consumer waste, processed chlorine free and new
Leaf Legac Offset made with 100% post-consumer waste, processed chlorine free. By using
this environmentally friendly paper, Lantern Books saved the following resources:

trees	water	energy	solid waste	greenhouse gases
6 fully grown	1,992 gallons	5 million BTUs	428 pounds	1,195 pounds

Calculated based on research done by Environmental Defense and other members of the Paper Task Force.

© New Leaf Paper   Visit us in cyberspace at www.newleafpaper.com or call 1-888-989-5323

An Expensive Way to Make Bad People Worse

Praise for *The Way of the Prisoner*

"A marvelous treatise on a valuable tradition of contemplative prayer, this is also a moving account of the author's experience of incarceration and spiritual renewal." —*The Other Side*

"Soering has used his own life story, from despair to enlightenment, to create a spiritual manual for anyone interested in meditation or Christian contemplation as a means of overcoming adversity." —*Daily Progress*

"In lucid prose . . . the transformative, life-saving efficacy of Centering Prayer and Centering Practice [is] described throughout this powerful book. . . . [O]f great help to anyone desiring to pray contemplatively." —*Monastic Interreligious Dialogue Bulletin*

". . . [A] thoughtful exploration. . . . [B]y following the Way of the Prisoner, one enters a long journey of discovery that ends with the joy of realization and closeness to God." —*Catholic Peace Voice*

"The book's glimpses into prison life are fascinating, absorbing and sad. . . . The mystical insight Soering relates will strike fellow contemplatives as true to their own experiences of God's vastness." —*Celebration/National Catholic Reporter*

"A contemporary contribution to the history of Christian thought that stretches from the Pauline prison epistles to the writing of Dietrich Bonhoeffer and Martin King. The context of being in jail seems to evoke a certain degree of depth and candor that is not always present in other religious literature. I would encourage the reader not to miss the spiritual autobiography of this prisoner." —*Eastern Shore Episcopalian*

To Anne-Claire, in memoriam, *and Ann*

Acknowledgments

Special thanks go to my research elves, Dick Busch, Lewise Busch, Mary Edwards, Sarah Gallogly, Tom Keating and Stan Lloyd; my technical support team, Wayne Carter and Meredith Sweet; DWC and LHC Designworks, for graphics support; and, as always, my "midwife," Ann Rainey. I could not even have attempted this essay without their active help and encouragement. Any mistakes of fact or errors in tone are, of course, entirely my responsibility, not theirs.

Table of Contents

FOREWORD

Jens Soering is a brilliant observer of the world around him—a world he manages to see with insight and clarity from behind penitentiary walls.

During the early years of his confinement, Soering decided to call on spiritual resources within himself to avoid being destroyed by the prospect of a lifetime in prison. He did so in a way that eventually became a gift to us all—in the form of his earlier book, *The Way of the Prisoner*, a text that is on its way to becoming a contemplative classic.

And now it becomes clear that, in the process, Soering discovered a gift for luminous commentary on social issues as well. Unsurprisingly, it took him hardly any time at all to get into perspective the futility and the danger of America's tragic addiction to imprisonment. In *An Expensive Way to Make Bad People Worse*, he has written a galvanizing essay on the subject. I have read extensively about our country's huge and still growing correctional crisis, but nothing that has had the impact of Soering's overwhelming assembly of information and his persuasive presentation of the facts.

When I began my first job in the field of corrections

more than fifty years ago, I hardly anticipated that as the time came for me to more or less fold my tent, I would be feeling a heavy sense of disillusionment. In choosing a career I had been prompted by a certain measure of idealism, as had many of my colleagues of that era. How could any of us have known that by the mid-1970s the field of endeavor we had chosen would be in the process of marginalizing all notions of hope, imagination and compassion, or that due to the politics of that time (aided and abetted by some carelessly reached conclusions within the academic community) the very concept of rehabilitation would be viewed as discredited? The most cynical among us would not have predicted that the imprisonment function of the criminal justice system in America would have spiraled down into hardly more than human warehousing. The idea of more than two million people in American jails and penitentiaries would have been beyond the imagination of any of us.

But this is what has happened, and Soering's lucid commentary lays out both the implications of it all and the alternatives. Unfortunately, this book could lead at least some correctional officials to mark the author as a troublemaker, and so it is worth emphasizing here that Soering does not attack the concept of imprisonment or those who must administer prisons. He offers, instead, promising ways to improve lives and control crime more cost-effectively. For this he is to be commended.

While *An Expensive Way to Make Bad People Worse* illuminates a tragic state of affairs, it is at heart a hopeful book. Soering has observed that opinion makers and politicians, on the right and on the left, are beginning to see the expensive folly of our country's over-reliance on imprisonment. My hope is that this important book will help to accelerate the ongoing change of direction in criminal justice policy.

By giving us this guide to a better future, Soering has brought a ray of hope to an old ex-warden who has been heartsick over the regression that has occurred in the field of corrections over the past twenty-five years.

Charles Campbell, Director,
Alaska Department of Corrections, Retired

INTRODUCTION

On January 21, 2004, a miracle happened in Washington DC: Jamie Fellner of Human Rights Watch and Chuck Colson of Prison Fellowship Ministries found themselves publicly agreeing with one another. What brought these two representatives of the far left and the far right together for a unique moment of amity and concord? President George W. Bush's proposal for a prisoner re-entry program, which both Fellner and Colson showered with praise after its announcement during the State of the Union address the previous evening.

"This year, some 600,000 inmates will be released from prison back into society," the President told the country. "We know from long experience that if they can't find work, or a home, or help, they are much more likely to commit more crimes and return to prison." His solution? A $300 million program to provide "job retraining, transitional housing and mentoring services from religious and secular organizations."

No wonder Fellner and Colson found themselves on the same side of this issue. In fact, when it comes to the problem of reintegrating former convicts, even John Kerry agrees with George Bush: "All of our communities benefit when ex-offenders, who have paid their debt to society, get the help they need to avoid returning to a life of crime," his "Agenda for Urban America" announced during the 2004 general election. What Bush and Kerry have begun to address here is this country's ever-deepening prison crisis, of which the problem of released former inmates is only one symptom. And that Republican–Democratic consensus spells new hope for all Americans concerned about crime and public safety.

But wait: is there really a national crisis in crime control? According to the Bureau of Justice Statistics, the crime rate hit a thirty-year low in 2003, so all would seem to be well with the world. That same year, however, the US prison population rose another 2.9%, reaching a record 2.1 million. In one state, the Commonwealth of Virginia, crime has *fallen* by 25% since 1993, while the number of jail inmates has risen 83% and the number of penitentiary inmates has grown by 136%. Less crime, but more prisoners—a troubling trend that has enormous political, fiscal and even moral implications.

For one thing, a great many tax dollars are at stake. The operating costs for this country's state and federal prisons and jails rose from $49 billion to $57 billion between 1999 and 2001, the last year for which figures are available, while America's correctional population has grown between 2.6 and 3.6% each year since 1999. In this age of burgeoning budget deficits at every level of government, citizens deserve to know—and, indeed, should question—whether they are getting their money's worth.

"Every time you build a prison, you close a school," Victor Hugo noted long ago. So while correctional budgets grew 30% between 1987 and 1998, elementary and high school expenditures dropped 1.2% and university spending fell by 18.2%. California built twenty-one pen-

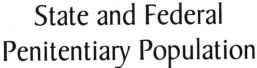

State and Federal Penitentiary Population

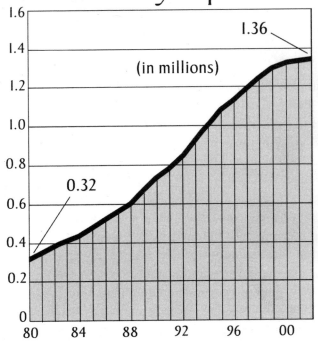

1.36

0.32

(in millions)

The figures above do not include inmates of jails, military brigs, or juvenile detention centers.

Source: Bureau of Justice Statistics

> Between 1984 and 1994, corrections spending in New York state increased by $761 million, while spending on state colleges and universities fell by $615 million. In 1995, the fifty states combined for the first time spent more on prisons than colleges—a trend that has accelerated since then.

itentiaries but only one university between 1984 and 1994 and pays its prison guards $10,000 more per year than its public school teachers. In New York, the corrections complex now consumes more state funds than any other government agency, including the once-cherished SUNY (State University of New York) system. Even little Virginia's prison department has become that state's largest public sector employer, at a time when K–12 education faces a $1 billion shortfall and public colleges require $400 million—in both cases, simply to meet current needs, not to expand programs. Given the very real and very painful budgetary trade-offs involved, it is only fair to inquire whether America's jails and penitentiaries really produce social benefits that exceed those of a similar investment in education.

A Fresh Perspective

This question deserves in-depth discussion, a serious public debate that I hope to encourage with this essay. What I bring to the table is a unique perspective that may help shed new light on the complex issues involved:

- I have made a serious amateur's study of criminology and

penology, and I have published one book and a number of articles in national magazines on these subjects.

- I am a prison inmate who has served eighteen years of two life terms for double murder. My insider's view of the criminal mind and penitentiary life allows me to put flesh on the dry skeleton of criminologists' statistics and, at least in some cases, to answer questions raised by the academics' numbers. Why, for instance, do 67.5% of all inmates released from prison re-offend? How can so many of them fail to learn their lesson? Below I will introduce you to the men I live with in "the big house," and that mystery will perhaps be solved.

- Finally, I also happen to be a citizen of Germany, a country that handles criminal justice issues very differently from the US. In fact, all the nations of the industrialized world, without exception, approach crime and prisons in a way that is diametrically opposite to America's, uniformly seeking to lower, not raise, correctional populations. And the results they achieve, as measured by their crime rates, are no worse than this country's—at vastly lower cost. So perhaps my international perspective can be of help as America begins to review its policies in this area.

A Moral Dimension

While this essay will focus primarily on the fiscal impact and effectiveness of current penological practices in the US, we must not forget that these matters also have a significant moral dimension. America prides itself on being the land of the free and the home of the brave, so it really does matter how many of its own citizens this nation deprives of their freedom. To deny another human being his or her liberty is a fearsome punishment indeed, as I can personally attest.

> "One reason we cannot stop crime in the United States is because many elements of the crime problem we believe to be true simply are not. Because of the way crime is presented in the media, crime events become distorted and are given unprecedented social consideration. These myths help to sustain our views of crime, criminals and the system as a whole."
>
> **Nancy E. Marion**,
> *A History of Federal Crime Control Initiatives*

But the act of incarceration has consequences for the jailer as well as for the jailed. When you consent to the use of your tax dollars for the purpose of caging your fellow man or woman, you assume responsibility for what is done with your money and in your name: the intentional infliction of pain in the name of justice. This moral aspect is rarely considered in public discussions of law and order policies, and I will not spend much time on it here. But as we review budgetary and criminological issues, let us keep in mind that money is not the only thing at stake when it comes to imprisoning your fellow man or woman.

Much of the difficulty in arriving at a rational, effective approach to matters of criminal justice stems from the myths on this subject that have taken hold in the public consciousness. What is considered fact or common sense is often wrong, sometimes wildly so. To correct some of these misperceptions, we will examine a number of these myths in an attempt to discover the nature of the fire beneath all that smoke.

MYTH NO. 1:

There is no problem.

As the introduction to this essay noted, the US crime rate recently reached a thirty-year low. The obvious conclusion is that the war on crime is being won, that there is no problem with America's approach to this issue. So what if we're building ever more prisons and the bills for all those jails turn out to be a little higher than expected? At least the nation's streets are safer.

What this argument, this myth, overlooks is both the expense and the sustainability of the current lull in the war on crime. The United States has indeed returned to crime rates not seen since the 1970s, but at rates of incarceration *seven times* as high as then: from just under 100 per 100,000 behind bars thirty years ago to 715 per 100,000 today. So the most that can be said is that America is doing no worse, at seven times the price.

And that price is not inconsiderable. Already 5.6 million adults in this country either are now or at one time have been in jail, and 11.3% of all males born in 2001 can expect to go to prison at some point in their lives. In addition to the cost of housing all these inmates, government budgets are further burdened by welfare payments to convicts' children (even today there are 1.5 million such boys

> While only 4.6% of the global population lives in the US, 22% of the world's prisoners are in American jails and penitentiaries.

and girls) and by reduced tax revenues due to the much lower incomes of employees with criminal records. Mass incarceration is by no means a cheap solution to the problem of crime.

An International Perspective

Nor does it appear to be the only solution, judging by the penological practices of every single other industrialized nation in the world. From Japan's low of 45 per 100,000 to England's high of 143 per 100,000, these countries all imprison their felons at much lower rates than does the US. Yet these nations achieve the same results as America in terms of crime control.

Repeated studies have established that industrialized countries experience surprisingly uniform rates of crime victimization: 21 to 24%. Even culturally and racially very homogenous nations like Finland only deviate by two percentage points from this figure, so it appears to be a given—an unalterable concomitant of advanced economic development. And the US victimization rate consistently matches the average rate of all industrialized countries.

The exception to this general rule is crimes involving the use of guns, which are far more widely available in this country than any other. For instance, the overall American murder rate is 5.6 times the rate in England and Wales, but factoring out firearm homicides, the US rate is only 2.4

times as high. And while Canadian rates for burglary and assault *without* guns are virtually identical to their American counterparts, there are only one eighth as many assaults *with* firearms to the north.

So—with the important exception of gun-related crimes—American crooks turn out to be no more dangerous than English or Canadian ones; only the governmental response to their illicit activity differs dramatically. According to Baroness Vivian Stern, an internationally recognized criminal justice expert and member of Britain's House of Lords, "a group of English-speaking countries—Canada, the . . . United Kingdom, Australia and New Zealand—are [all] moving toward an intensification of rehabilitation efforts . . . linking activities in prison to reintegration in the community." My own country's parliament, the Bundestag, is currently considering a Justice Ministry proposal to dramatically reduce the incarceration rate of 96 per 100,000 by making a full 20% of all criminal defendants eligible for community service instead of prison. The working title of this initiative is "intelligent punishment."

A Personal Perspective

At the very beginning of my long prison career, I spent three years and eight months in four different English penitentiaries, fighting extradition back to the US. So I had plenty of opportunity to observe the European criminal mind up close, before coming to Virginia for my introduction to its American counterpart. And I can assure you that British killers and thieves are no less murderous and rapacious than US killers and thieves. If anything, the Brits were worse than the Yanks from my personal point of view: English inmates broke my wrist on two occasions (in 1986

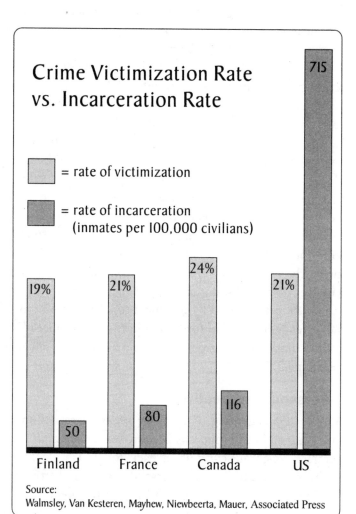

Crime Victimization Rate vs. Incarceration Rate

= rate of victimization

= rate of incarceration
(inmates per 100,000 civilians)

	Finland	France	Canada	US
rate of victimization	19%	21%	24%	21%
rate of incarceration	50	80	116	715

Source:
Walmsley, Van Kesteren, Mayhew, Niewbeerta, Mauer, Associated Press

> "The degree of civilization in a society can be judged by entering its prisons."
>
> **Fyodor Dostoyevsky**, *The House of the Dead*

and 1989), but only one American prisoner attempted to rape me (in 1991). In any case, I can point to no reason why Virginian criminals should be locked up at five or six times the rate of London crooks.

When I came to Virginia in 1990, this state's Department of Corrections housed roughly 9,000 inmates, whereas today it holds just over 35,000. So I have also had an opportunity to experience firsthand a good portion of America's experiment with mass imprisonment, the thirty-year growth of the incarceration rate from 100 to 715 per 100,000. And over the years, I noticed a number of significant shifts in the types of criminals in the cells around mine.

Compared to twelve or thirteen years ago, I now see many more very young *and* very old prisoners: juveniles sent to adult penitentiaries, and old-timers who in the past would have been granted parole. Also, I now see many more convicts serving time for drug-related offenses: between 1991 and 1997, the percentage of state prisoners incarcerated for such crimes rose from 21.3 to 57.9%, with similar growth rates in the federal system. Interestingly enough, "young bucks," "old heads" and drug users—though not dealers—were entirely absent from the English penitentiaries in which I served time.

What I never met in prison, even once, was one of the "super-predators" of whom conservative criminologist John J. DiIulio Jr. warned so loudly and persistently ten to fifteen years ago. These mythic monsters—"deviant, delinquent, and criminal . . . chaotic, dysfunctional, fatherless, godless and jobless," according to DiIulio—served to justify much of the expansion of the American correctional systems to its current enormous size. But not even the inmate who tried to rape me more than a dozen years ago fits this description: he was an "old head" who may have seen *me* as a young "super-predator."

A Conservative Perspective

As I will argue throughout this essay and especially in Myth No. 6 and the Conclusion, classic fiscal conservatism is the key both to understanding the enormity of the budgetary problem created by over-incarceration *and* to solving that problem. Indeed, Republican politicians and commentators—not liberals—are in the forefront of the movement to bring some much-needed sanity to this country's penal policies. Conservative editorialist Cal Thomas put the case in eloquently simple terms in a recent column:

> After two decades of being "tough on crime" by "locking them up and throwing away the key"—to recall two of the politically effective slogans of the past—the bill has come due. Many states have become incapable or unwilling to pay the cost of housing record numbers of inmates. . . .
>
> What are taxpayers getting for their money? They get a false sense of security, as if putting current criminals behind bars ensures there won't be future criminals. . . . We should be focusing on restitution. . . .
>
> Republicans, who were behind many of these "tough on crime" laws, have an opportunity to fight crime in ways that will actually work and save tax-

payers lots of money. That is supposed to be the Republican way. It is certainly the only way that will work.

MYTH NO. 2:

They may be expensive,
but at least prisons prevent crime.

As in the case of Myth No. 1, this bit of apparent common sense carries a certain superficial plausibility: crooks cannot break the law so long as they remain behind bars, right? But not even conservative criminologists like James Q. Wilson believe that prison prevents crime; that is why even he admits, "very large increases in the prison population can only produce modest reductions in crime rates." The British government's Home Office agrees, concluding that a 25% rise in the number of inmates would lower crime rates by only 1%. In one well-known California study, the 300% growth of that state's penitentiary system in the 1980s was shown to reduce non-violent crimes like burglary marginally, but rapes and murders hardly at all. "SPP [state prison population] changes have little or no impact on murder, rape or assault," other researchers confirmed. Even the US Department of Justice realizes that locking up as many felons as possible "does not appear to achieve large reductions in crime [but] can cause enormous increases in prison populations."

Ironically, the Justice Department reached this conclusion *in 1983*, near the beginning of the huge expansion of

America's correctional system. But all those jails were built anyway. And if you build it, they will come.

The Criminal Mind

Why do they—that is, criminals—keep coming to prison in spite of the fact that they should know better? In other words, *why* does deterrence not work? To answer that question, let us examine some statistical data describing the typical American convict:

- 20% of US inmates are so seriously deranged that even prison medical departments must acknowledge that they are mentally ill.
- 37% of inmates were under the influence of alcohol at the time they committed their crimes, and another 33% were under the influence of drugs.
- 19% of prisoners are completely illiterate, and 40% are functionally illiterate.
- On average, convicts' IQ scores are 8 to 10 points lower than the general population's.
- 38% of arrests nationally are of young males aged 15 to 24.

In other words, prison does not deter crime because criminals are too crazy, too drunk, too high, too uneducated, too unintelligent and too young to fully comprehend what they were doing at the time they broke the law.

Of course the factors cited above do not excuse felons' behavior. But we can certainly now understand why making penitentiary life even harder, or lengthening sentences further, or even publicly executing petty thieves would not reduce crime. Politicians and judges may think they are "sending a message" by toughening laws, but their intended audience is not listening.

> "[Prisons] do succeed in punishing, but they do not deter. They make successful reintegration in the community unlikely. They change the committed offender, but the change is likely to be more negative than positive."
>
> **US National Commission on Criminal Justice Standards and Goals**, 1973—i.e., at the very beginning of the great prison building boom

I can confirm this from personal experience: to the best of my knowledge, not one of my associates behind bars undertook a rational cost-benefit analysis before breaking the law, mostly because they were stoned, pickled or stupid at *all* times, not just the time of their offense. Perhaps the only exception to this rule is myself: I actually made a careful calculation of how much time I would serve in which country if I, a German citizen, became an accomplice to double murder in Virginia. But I was only eighteen years old and wildly misinformed about the state of the law, and I made a terrible mistake.

Age is, in fact, the primary statistical predictor of criminal behavior. To effectively prevent crime, one need only take all seventeen- and eighteen-year-old males out of circulation for a year or two; those are the peak ages for committing robbery, aggravated assault and burglary. Perhaps the draft, which formerly served to temporarily incapacitate crime-prone teenagers, should be revived today in altered form—as a year of civilian national service, for example.

The Perpetual Prisoner Machine

Instead of letting youngsters fill sandbags in the military or renovate inner-city housing in a mandatory youth job corps, however, this country now sends its errant teenagers to jail and, after a decade or two, releases them back to the streets with a criminal record that permanently impairs their ability to earn a legal living. It is at this point that America's perpetual prisoner machine jumps into operation, producing more inmates at a *rising* rate. In the following paragraphs, I will have to cite a great many numbers, but I ask you to bear with me and trust that our destination is worth the somewhat arduous trip.

Excluding military brigs and juvenile detention centers, the US houses 2.1 million inmates in its prisons and jails. Of these convicts, 625,000 are released each year—not because they are paroled, since parole has effectively been abolished even for those technically still eligible, but because their sentences are over. Although 67.5% of released inmates are re-arrested within three years, only 51.8% are sent back to prison: a total of 323,750 men and women. One hundred and sixty-five thousand, or 26.4%, return to the penitentiary for so-called "technical violations" of post-release rules, like failure to attend drug counseling, while 158,750, or 25.4%, come back for new crimes. In addition to those prison sentences for former inmates, this nation's courts impose another 300,000 terms of incarceration for new offenders who have never been behind bars until now. So, while 625,000 convicts are *released* each year, a fresh crop of 623,750 criminals *enters* US penitentiaries: 165,000 violators, 158,750 recidivists and 300,000 first-time felons.

These numbers would balance out, if it were not for

first-time "technical" violators of *suspended* prison sentences.

There are at this time 3,932,751 Americans on probation, 14% of whom break the terms of their suspended sentences and also enter the correctional system each year: an additional 546,000 inmates. We have, however, "counted" most of these incoming convicts already, somewhere among the 323,750 former prisoners returning to jail and the 300,000 new felons cited earlier. What we do not know—because the Bureau of Justice Statistics does not tell us—is how many of the 546,000 probationers-turned-inmates are "technical violators" who have never been to jail or prison before—i.e., who received only suspended sentences at their original trials and are now making their very first trip behind bars for *non-felonious* forms of misbehavior. *These* new prisoners have not yet been "counted" anywhere in the above groups of inmates entering jail.

If only 10% of those 546,000 fell into this category, then we would have an extra 54,600 "fresh fish," or newcomers to "the big house," each and every year. And it so happens that this figure accounts *precisely* for the 2.6% growth of the US jail and penitentiary population in the mid-2001 to mid-2002 accounting period (reported in mid-2003): 2.1 million x 2.6% = 54,600!

Corrections officials are fully aware, by the way, that technical violations of probation sentences play a pivotal role in America's prison crisis. "I think every state in the country has recognized this as a growing problem. It's a driving force on the prison population everywhere," says Richard P. Kern, Director of Virginia's Criminal Sentencing Commission. Since 2001, one third of that state's prison growth consisted specifically of technical probation viola-

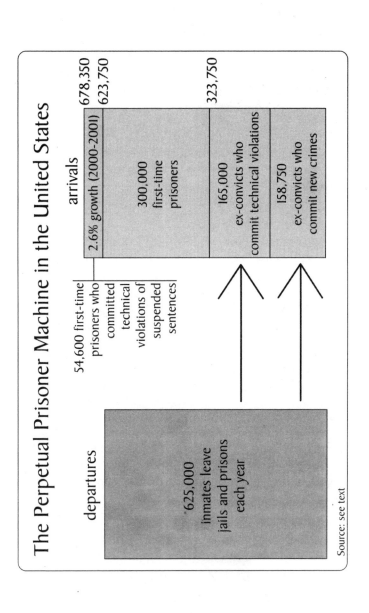

The Perpetual Prisoner Machine in the United States

arrivals

678,350
623,750

2.6% growth (2000-2001)

300,000
first-time
prisoners

323,750

165,000
ex-convicts who
commit technical violations

158,750
ex-convicts who
commit new crimes

54,600 first-time
prisoners who
committed
technical
violations of
suspended
sentences

departures

625,000
inmates leave
jails and prisons
each year

Source: see text

In Virginia, 46% of all probation violators committed only "technical" violations, and 10% of that state's total prison population now consists of such inmates.

tors—new convicts who "failed drug tests or missed meetings with probation officers," but committed no actual felonies.

So America's correctional system has apparently reached "critical mass." Much as a sufficiently large pile of fissionable material produces its own, self-sustaining chain reaction, this country's penitentiaries now produce enough excess inmates to keep growing indefinitely. Each year, a few tens of thousands more enter than exit—with no end in sight.

The Future

Those additional ex-felons will in time have a growing impact on this nation's crime rate, of course, as more and more of them commit new offenses during their brief vacations from jail.

"No one is more dangerous than a criminal who has no incentive to straighten himself out while in prison and who returns to society without a supervised treatment plan," notes Department of Justice consultant Joan Petersilia in a new study on recidivism. Yet it is precisely this type of person that the US correctional system is even now producing in ever-larger numbers: a different kind of "super-predator" than John J. DiIulio Jr. imagined, but no less frightening.

As the British government found in a 1990 "white

paper," prison is "an expensive way to make bad people worse." "The American incarceration rate is . . . the highest in the world, *but it has not made the United States a safer place to live*," the Correctional Service of Canada noted recently (italics mine). It is the ineffectiveness of this country's penological practice that explains why, "among mainstream politicians and commentators in Western Europe, . . . the criminal justice system of the United States is an inexplicable deformity [that] arouses incredulity and incomprehension."

Perhaps the time has come to stop doing what evidently does *not* work and to try something else: crime prevention, for instance—the subject of our next myth.

MYTH NO. 3:

Crime prevention does not work.

There is, in fact, considerable truth to this myth: as we saw earlier with Myth No. 1, all industrialized nations experience crime victimization rates of 21 to 24%, so no one has found the perfect recipe for preventing all illegal activity. Apparently, a certain level of lawlessness simply has to be accepted as the standard, international price of living in an economically developed society. This is a difficult concept to accept for Americans, who are used to thinking in terms of total victory in all their wars. But the war on crime is no more likely to end with perfect peace and flower-strewn streets than, say, the war in Iraq.

What is really at issue both in the Middle East and in America's streets and courtrooms is effective problem management: minimizing the harm done to the innocent, lowering the intensity of the conflict, containing the threat, and luring the next generation into compliance with authority. This is face-to-face, long-term work, but it can be effective if pursued patiently. Contrary to popular myth, we already know exactly what works and what does not when it comes to crime prevention.

Ineffective Measures

What does not work is threats and preaching, as anyone with even the slightest familiarity with teenagers in or out of prison knows. Participants in the first "Scared Straight" program, for instance, were *more* likely to end up behind bars than a control group of non-participants; and even the US Department of Justice admits that having policemen lecture teens about drugs in "Project DARE" is completely ineffective.

So why do such programs continue to enjoy popular support? Perhaps because they satisfy an atavistic need to see delinquent youngsters get their comeuppance at the hands of someone who, finally, is stronger than they are: convicts and cops. Unfortunately, at-risk youths do not enjoy being bullied any more than you do, and they respond to being menaced by becoming more menacing themselves.

The cells around mine are filled with graduates of boot camps and "Scared Straight"-type programs. In conversations with me, they pride themselves on having survived these trials-by-fire and emerging even tougher than before. "The man" pushed them to the limit, but afterwards—*afterwards!*—it was their turn to get some "get-back." On civilians like you, of course.

Improving Children's Lives

Here is what *does* work in crime prevention: improving the lives of poor children while they are growing up.

In 1984, the RAND Corporation—an institution not known to be politically progressive—conducted an in-depth study of the Chicago Area Project (CAP), after fifty years of continuous operation. CAP organizes slum residents into community committees that work personally with local youths in trouble, improve the physical appearance of neighborhoods, and provide recreational facilities for youngsters. This, not threats or lectures, proved to be "effective in reducing rates of juvenile delinquency."

In the Perry Preschool Program, 123 "borderline educable mentally retarded" children from an extreme low-income black neighborhood in Ypsilanti, Michigan, were enrolled in preschool two years early and visited by their teachers at home once a week for two years—nothing more. Twenty-seven years later, participants were found to be only one-fifth as likely as a control group of non-participants to become habitual criminals, and only one-fourth as likely to be arrested for a drug-related crime. Similar results were found in Syracuse University's Family Development Research Program, another long-term pilot study that emphasized helping parents raise their children while they were still very young. Again: we know what works.

Poverty

Why do initiatives like those above succeed in preventing crime? Because they attack the root causes of crime. The surprise here is that we actually know fairly precisely what those causes are. They are no mystery, and they could be addressed nationally, as they already have been in local programs like CAP.

When I walk out of my cell into my housing unit's day-room, I do not see a great many people like myself: a former middle-class white kid, now approaching middle age. What I see, almost without exception, are poor blacks, poor whites and poor Hispanics. Now, *either* it is just a coincidence that all these people happened to be living in slums and trailer parks when they used their free will to choose to break the law. *Or* maybe—just maybe—there really is a link between poverty and criminal behavior.

> Youngsters matched with mentors (e.g., Big Brothers/
> Big Sisters) are 46% less likely to use drugs, 27% less
> likely to begin drinking, one third less likely to commit
> assault, and half as likely to skip school.

That idea is anathema in America, of course, because if low incomes and social deprivation really do lead to increased rates of lawlessness, then crime might be reduced by redistributing some wealth. But among social scientists, the connection between poverty and criminality has not been in dispute for a long time: a 1981 meta-analysis of 224 previous studies "concluded rather convincingly that members of lower social classes were indeed more prone to commit crime," a finding confirmed by later researchers. So could crime prevention be as simple as raising the incomes of America's poor?

Some data indicates that indeed it might be. A 1996/97 study of AFDC (Aid to Families with Dependent Children) payments in 140 metropolitan areas—controlling for all sorts of variables, accounting for all kinds of regional differences—found that the higher the welfare payments were, the lower the burglary and homicide rates fell. And in international comparisons, we again see that countries spending 12 to 14% of their Gross Domestic Product (GDP) on welfare have lower rates of violent crime in particular than the US, which spends only 4% of its GDP on welfare.

Any penitentiary warden can confirm this phenomenon. Neither more prison guards nor tougher rules keep convicts in line behind bars, but the judicious apportionment of menial jobs paying 23 to 45 cents per hour (in Virginia penitentiaries) does. Inmates who have no other source of

Welfare vs. Prison and Other Housing Costs

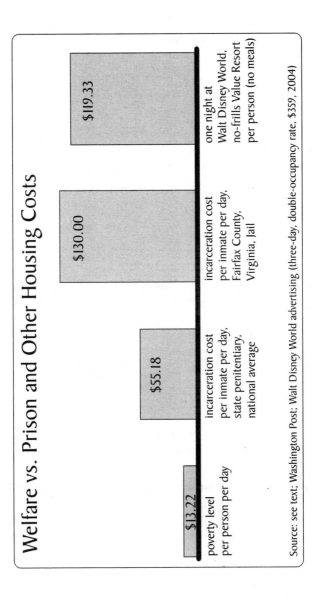

$13.22	$55.18	$130.00	$119.33
poverty level per person per day	incarceration cost per inmate per day, state penitentiary, national average	incarceration cost per inmate per day, Fairfax County, Virginia, Jail	one night at Walt Disney World, no-frills Value Resort per person (no meals)

Source: see text; Washington Post; Walt Disney World advertising (three-day, double-occupancy rate, $359, 2004) income can easily be seduced into compliance by this method, no matter how tough they pretend to be.

If that sounds terribly cynical, consider why *you* obey your society's rules on the other side of the razor wire fence. You pay your taxes and obey the speed limit because you have something to lose—not because you actually enjoy giving your money to the IRS or driving your BMW far below its capabilities. When the poor respond to financial incentives by reducing their illegal activity, they are simply obeying the same proven rules of micro-economics in capitalist societies that govern your behavior.

The official poverty level for a family of three is $14,480 per year, or $13.22 per person per day for *everything*: rent, utilities, clothes, food, transportation, medical expenses, education—*everything*. According to the US Census Bureau, 3.8 million families are so poor that some members actually had to skip meals for lack of funds, and another 11 million families reported being afraid that they would run out of food. Why is it considered morally offensive and economically unwise in this country to give a poor person a few dollars more than $13.22 per day, but ethically appropriate and fiscally sensible to incarcerate a poor person at an average cost of $55.18 per day?

Fatherless Families

Before liberals celebrate research findings on the link between poverty and crime, however, we had better examine *how* low incomes lead to illegal behavior. It turns out that conservatives are right to lay the finger of blame on dysfunctional family structures—specifically absent fathers. For those 36% of all American children who grow up in single-parent families, the future looks grim indeed.

Both juvenile delinquency and poverty have been consistently associated with fatherless homes since the early nineteenth century. But it is important to note that it is *the absence of the father* that is the underlying cause of the other two phenomena. Because there is only one breadwinner in the house, children raised by their mother alone are six times more likely to be poor than similarly situated children raised by both parents. And because there is only one adult to supervise and role-model kids, children (overwhelmingly sons) raised without fathers make up 60% of rapists, 72% of adolescent murderers, and 70% of all long-term inmates.

Fathers cannot simply be forced to act responsibly toward their offspring, of course, so the question becomes: what can be done to help poor single mothers raise their children so they are less likely to turn to crime later? One answer appears to be something as simple as home-visiting by public health care workers—as in a pilot program called PEIP, in Elmira, New York—or teachers—as in the Perry Preschool Program, discussed above. According to another RAND Corporation study, parent training and early intervention can reduce crime four or five times as effectively as California's "three strikes" law. So with a little help, even an absent father need not spell doom for a child in poverty.

In my neighborhood—the penitentiary—practically everyone my age or younger grew up in a single-parent home on the seediest side of town. A young man I met recently in an inmate meditation group is typical: he came to prison at age fifteen (because he was tried as an adult) and now, at age twenty-three, he is about to finish his sentence and return "home." But his mother, who is only thirty-eight herself, is in the process of dying from the effects of a lifetime of drug abuse. So he has no home to return to, no family or community connections of any kind. A few weeks from now, he will step through the prison gate into a world he last saw as a child and where he knows no one.

What continually surprises me is how many young men like this one tell me that they want to leave their lives of crime behind. In fact, one federal study found that over half of all youths who join gangs tried to quit, and 79% said they would leave if given "a second chance in life." As far as I can tell, many of my fellow prisoners never had their first chance, never mind their second.

Abuse

Growing up poor and fatherless unfortunately carries an additional danger that can heighten still further a child's chances of later becoming a criminal: abuse, physical or sexual. Among underclass families, reported cases of mal-treatment are three times as frequent as among higher income groups, and such children are then twice as likely to be involved in serious or violent delinquency. Later, as adults, victims of abuse are 38% more likely to be arrested for violent crime, with the result that 16.1% of male prison inmates and 57.2% of female prison inmates report having been physically or sexually maltreated while growing up—rates far higher than in the general population.

Among convicts, discussing past abuse directly is absolutely taboo, of course. But if the dayroom TV is tuned to the local news when the arrest of some particularly odi-ous juvenile offender is reported, one can sometimes hear prisoners discuss how the youngster in question would have behaved himself if only he had been "whooped" the way they were "whooped" by their parents. The idea that the leather-belt beatings they suffered as children may have contributed to their own later acts of violence does not

> "We know full well that the most serious and intractable types of crime have their roots in the very child welfare problems that are neglected as we trash through one ineffective war on crime after another."
>
> **Brian Vila**, "Could We Break the Crime Control Paradox," annual meeting of the American Society of Criminology, 1994

seem to occur to these inmates. So, after their release, they will presumably also "whoop" their own offspring into temporary submission.

The Future

What, then, does the future hold for America's children? For 1.5 million of them, it holds a childhood growing up in single-parent homes, because their fathers or mothers are behind bars—an interesting side effect of mass incarceration that will have predictably tragic consequences. According to the US Census Bureau, 17.2% of all children—12.2 million boys and girls—now live below the poverty level of $14,480 per year for a family of three. And out of thirty-two states evaluated under the Child and Family Services Review for their "ability to protect children from child abuse," twenty-eight states failed either all seven or six out of seven criteria. This, when there are over one million substantiated cases of child abuse each year.

So America is readying a fresh batch of prospective convicts to feed to its jails and penitentiaries. But as we have seen above, at least some of those literally millions of lives could be saved instead of thrown away.

The key concept to understand in this context is that both prison and welfare are responses to *poverty*, since poverty is the link that connects crime to the associated phenomena of fatherless families and child abuse. Of course both welfare and prison are necessary and complementary components of any effective anti-poverty policy. What has happened in the United States over the last thirty years, however, is that the carrot has been almost totally eliminated in favor of more and larger sticks. "A growing prison system was what we had *instead* of an anti-poverty policy, instead of an employment policy, instead of a comprehensive drug-treatment or mental health policy," says criminologist Elliott Currie.

In Europe, by contrast, social policies are designed around "the internationally recognized principle of using custodial sentences only when strictly necessary," according to the Danish Prison and Probation Service. This emphasis on welfare over prisons in the anti-poverty "mix" has the pleasant side effect that only 4% of Danish and Norwegian children, and just 6% of French and German kids, grow up in poverty—as opposed to 22% of American children (by this study's definition of poverty, which is less than half the country's median income).

So the question becomes, where do you want your tax dollars to be invested: early on in the cycle, when they can still improve a child's life? Or at the end of the cycle, when all that is left is to lock the cell door after the horse of hope has bolted?

MYTH NO. 4:

Rehabilitation behind bars does not work.

Actually, I agree with this "myth" wholeheartedly—but for reasons other than those you might suspect. So let us take a closer look at the idea that prison cannot rehabilitate, to see what we can discover about the reality of correctional education and treatment.

For instance, how do we "know" that schooling and therapy—which have certainly improved the lives of millions of civilians—simply have no effect on prisoners? Are inmates just too stupid and too evil for education and treatment to help them, as they have helped you? Or are penitentiaries perhaps not giving convicts what you and I would recognize as real academic and vocational training, real psychosocial care?

The answer is, a bit of both. As we saw earlier, prisoners as a group have a host of enormous, interrelated problems: mental illness, alcohol and drug dependency, illiteracy, sub-average IQs, inadequate parenting, and a history of physical and/or sexual abuse. Just one of these deficiencies would be considered a serious handicap in your world, but the overwhelming majority of inmates are afflicted with several. To improve their ability to survive in a society without breaking the law would require intensive individual effort—a daunting task indeed.

Perhaps that is why this task is so infrequently attempted: only 6% of state penitentiary funding goes to in-prison rehabilitative programs. And what does that 6% look like in practice?

- Although one fifth of all convicts are certified mentally ill, 40% of jails and 17% of prisons do not even bother to test the mental health status of their inmates, never mind making any attempt at therapy. Iowa's correctional department provides only three psychiatrists for more than 8,000 prisoners, while Wyoming's state penitentiary has a single psychiatrist on duty—for two days each month. As a result of this lack of treatment, mentally ill inmates frequently stay in their prison's punishment blocks for years on end, according to a recent study of New York's Department of Correctional Services. Fully 25% of the inmates in that state's punitive segregation units are diagnosed as mentally ill, and half of those surveyed attempted to commit suicide while confined there.

- Only 14% of those prisoners who were drunk when they committed their crimes receive treatment for alcohol abuse behind bars; and just 18% of those convicts who were high at the time of their offense get drug therapy while incarcerated.

- Nearly two thirds of all prisoners cannot read and write, but only 23.4% participate—not complete, but just participate—in a GED/high school equivalency program during their incarceration.

- For youthful offenders—the sub-group of convicts most likely to respond to rehabilitative efforts—the situation is even worse: *half* of America's juvenile prisons do not

Annual cost of effective treatment program (per inmate, per year): $3,500. Resulting savings in first year after completion of treatment . . .

. . . in reduced crime: $5,000

. . . in reduced arrest and prosecution costs: $7,300

. . . in annual cost of incarceration (national average): $21,000

NET annual savings: $29,800

provide correctional education services that meet the requirements of state and federal law, and 90% of juveniles sent to adult prisons are released without a high school diploma or GED. Since only 4% of juvenile justice funding goes to aftercare treatment, these youthful offenders are not likely to get any help upon their return to society, either.

And, needless to say, neither juvenile prisoners nor adult convicts receive any kind of therapy anywhere for the physical and sexual abuse so many experienced as children, before coming to prison.

Education

During my eighteen years of incarceration, I have taken part in precisely one vocational training course— Introduction to Computers, lasting four months—and a grand total of three treatment programs, lasting twelve or fifteen hours each: Drug Abuse, "Breaking Barriers" and Anger Management.

Twenty years ago, I won a full academic scholarship to

one of the top ten universities in this country, but I could not continue my education in prison because college programs behind bars have now been cut almost entirely: from 350 in 1982 to no more than 12 in the entire United States in 2001. Thanks for this development must go to President Bill Clinton's elimination of Pell Grants for prisoners in 1994, after which virtually all states excluded inmates from state tuition grants as well.

The Drug Abuse, "Breaking Barriers" and Anger Management courses I was required to take were so breathtakingly unprofessional that I lack words to describe them. Perhaps the grammatically challenged author of one of the instructional booklets said it best: "Education yourself about anger." One of these programs was actually produced by an ex-convict who obviously had no psychological training whatsoever and simply exhorted us to think positive! For all of us inmate participants, it was overwhelmingly clear that the "free-worlders" who put these courses together could not care less if we learned anything. Of course, we all *did* learn something, an old lesson most of us had been taught many times before: that we are worthless and hopeless.

What is so infuriating about the neglect of correctional education in particular is that it *provably* reduces recidivism. Earning a GED while incarcerated lowers ex-offenders' chances of returning to jail by 25.9% compared to inmates who leave the penitentiary without a high school equivalency diploma. And in a 1991 (pre-Pell Grant abolition) study, those who completed a college degree program behind bars re-offended at nearly half the rate of those who began but did not finish their studies. In other words, with 625,000 inmates being released every year, this country could prevent *tens of thousands* of crimes *each*

Education and Recidivism in Virginia

Reincarceration rates of released inmates who, during their previous term of imprisonment, had ...

no educational programming: 49.1%

some education, but did not complete it: 38.2%

completed educational programming: 19.1%

Source: Virginia Department of Correctional Education

year, simply by hiring enough penitentiary teachers to meet currently unmet needs, and by requiring prisoners to earn a degree commensurate with their intellectual abilities—before returning to society. Now, *that* would be "tough on crime" indeed.

I have personally watched scores upon scores of seemingly unsalvageable convicts transform their lives through education, even with the very limited opportunities offered by underfunded correctional education departments. One of my acquaintances at my current prison, for instance, used to be the collection agent for this facility's chief gambling mafiosi, a real "gangsta" who made a point of enjoying his work. But then one day something changed. Today this former "super-predator" is a teacher's aide in the penitentiary computer class and gets embarrassed when I tease him about the "weak white boys" he used to beat down.

Due to funding cuts, however, the computer class teacher is sometimes forced to pay out of her own pocket for normal operating supplies like printer cartridges, and the entire program is in continual danger of being eliminated for budgetary reasons. California cut its correctional education expenditure by $46.2 million in the current fiscal year, and in Kansas's Ellsworth prison, GED classes have been cut in half and substance abuse courses eliminated entirely—to save money. No doubt funds will be found, however, when it comes time to re-incarcerate unrehabilitated prisoners who re-offend upon release.

Psychotherapy

In addition to the long record of effective rehabilitation established by academic and vocational training, there is now new evidence that intensive psychotherapy can reduce recidivism significantly in the most problematic sub-group

> "Treatment works."
>
> **State Representative Ray Allen**, R-Texas,
> Chairman of House Corrections Committee,
> in interview with Fort Worth *Star-Telegram*

of convicts: sex offenders. Here some context is necessary, however. Contrary to popular myth, only 17.3% of rapists and molesters actually commit a new *sex* crime after their release—not 80% or 90%, as even many law enforcement officials believe. That recidivism rate can be cut *nearly in half* to 9.9% through modern treatment methods, according to a major recent meta-analysis of therapeutic programs conducted by Canada's Solicitor General. Apparently, the key is to match the correct treatment technique to the specific type of offender, and especially to begin therapy early, since "attitudes that led to offending can become stronger, more virulent in prison."

The penitentiary in which I am presently housed is home to a cutting-edge pilot program called SORT (Sex Offender Residential Treatment), which offers roughly one hundred inmates intensive therapy in a community setting. From numerous conversations with program participants, I can only conclude that their sessions with the staff psychologists are extremely tough—anything but touchy-feely coddling. And this technique appears to work: after nearly three years of operation, not a single SORT graduate has committed a new sex crime.

Faith-Based Initiatives

Yet another successful approach to rehabilitation behind

bars focuses on faith. In the 1970s a Catholic evangelization initiative called Cursillo re-opened an old penitentiary called Humaita in the Brazilian state of Sao Paulo and operated it entirely along Christian lines—with an enormous reduction in recidivism rates. Chuck Colson's Prison Fellowship Ministries brought this idea to Texas, where their "InnerChange Freedom Initiative" prison achieved rates of re-offending of under 5%. In a study of a Prison Fellowship program in New York, participants recidivated at a rate of 14%, while 41% of a control group of non-participants re-offended.

There has been some controversy about the effectiveness claims made by InnerChange in Texas, and, as a Catholic, I am troubled that such programs preach only an extreme right-wing version of Protestantism, including a belief in "creationism." But these problems could be addressed through reform and ecumenical oversight and especially through more zeal on the part of mainline Protestants and Catholics. As I can attest through personal experience, the positive effect of religion on the lives of convicts is a very real phenomenon that should not be neglected in any coordinated rehabilitation approach.

On every penitentiary yard, one can always find clusters of prisoners praying and doing Bible studies, or performing *salaah* in the direction of Mecca. What I find especially interesting in this context is the self-policing function of these inmate faith groups: when one member commits a sin, the others do not automatically shun or expel him, but usually try to bring him back into the fold through scripturally based persuasion and exhortation. The offenders respond well to this approach because—as a few have told me privately—these convict religious groups are their first direct experience of belonging to a caring community, a "family."

Restorative Justice

For those not inclined to a life of faith, the experience of Britain's Restorative Prison Project offers hope through working for secular charities. At fifteen different English penitentiaries, from low to maximum security, inmates repair wheelchairs, transcribe Braille, recycle textiles and much else, in order to give back something of value to the society whose rules they have broken. All participants are volunteers, with long-term convicts being the most enthusiastic. Interestingly enough, 90% of the participants interviewed by the International Centre for Prison Studies in 2001 specifically wished their work to be credited not to themselves individually, but to inmates generally, in order to "change any negative opinions the community have of prisoners as a collective."

All Belgian penitentiaries have a "restorative justice counselor" on staff who develops restorative activities for inmates and facilitates communication between the offender and his or her victim, or the offender and the community. In the Netherlands, the Dutch Correctional Service prides itself on its "neighborhood approach" and its "cooperat[ion] with local partner organizations to foster the successful reintegration of prisoners." Comparison studies of the recidivism rates of participants in such programs versus non-participants are not available, for the simple reason that it would not occur to the correctional departments of other industrialized nations not to make at least some attempt to rehabilitate all of their inmates.

Reintegration

And that brings me to the first of my two fundamental objections to the idea of reforming convicts behind bars: rehabilitation is pointless without reintegration. The absolutely essential prerequisite for any educational or therapeutic program is the belief or at least hope in the participating inmates' minds that their lives can really change for the better, that the skills they are about to learn will help them achieve some measure of success upon release. But there is currently no way to convince prisoners to make this crucial leap of faith, because so many of our fellow convicts are recidivists who tell us in great detail about the nearly insurmountable obstacles we will face in the "free world."

Thanks to President Bill Clinton's Personal Responsibility and Work Opportunity Reconciliation Act of 1996, ex-felons with a drug conviction on their records—in other words, the majority of all released inmates—are now barred from food stamps, family welfare benefits and access to federally subsidized housing. Two years later the Higher Education Act of 1998 went on to exclude former drug offenders from student loans as well, leading to 9,000 denied applications in one year alone—from men and women who had served their time and now wanted to become more productive citizens.

"All the things they need to get their life started back [are] off limits, and there's nothing they can do about it. They wind up homeless, back on the streets," according to Amy Hirsch, author and attorney with Community Legal Service of Philadelphia. With no place left to turn, many ex-convicts suffer an ironic fate: an astonishing 43% of Washington DC's homicide *victims* in the first half of 2003

> "[Ex-offenders] are as much affected by the actions of government as any other citizen, and have as much of a right to participate in governmental decision-making. Furthermore, the denial of a right to vote to such persons is a hindrance to the efforts of society to rehabilitate former felons and convert them into law-abiding and productive citizens."
>
> **US Supreme Court Justice Thurgood Marshall**,
> in *Richardson v. Ramirez*

were people released from the DC jail or federal prison within the previous two years.

Even those former prisoners who do not end up on the streets encounter enormous resistance. As I write these lines, an acquaintance of mine is leaving this penitentiary upon completion of his sentence: a middle-aged white man with an intact family and a successful furniture store waiting for him. Two weeks ago, however, he received letters from his two major suppliers, informing him that they would no longer do business with his store if he resumed management in person. This morning, when I said goodbye to him, he seemed not joyful but scared.

A large part of the problem is that men and women like this acquaintance of mine are quite literally and legally second-class citizens who have no power to alter their lives. Over four million Americans, or 2.28% of the adult population of this country, are barred from voting even after their terms of incarceration have been completed, a policy known as felony disenfranchisement. By contrast, the great majority of industrialized countries allow not only ex-offenders but also prison inmates to vote; I personally received my own ballot for the German national election from the German Embassy in the summer of 2002, after having spent (at that time) sixteen years incarcerated in England and the US. In America, the national election of 2000 was almost certainly *decided* by felony disenfranchisement, since a full 827,000 Floridians—including 31.2% of African American men—were barred from the ballot box due to their past criminal records.

Rape

Apart from the enormous legal, social and political barriers to reintegration, former prisoners often have to cope with an even greater problem: the trauma of having been raped behind bars and the fact that they now have an HIV/AIDS infection. Former Virginia Attorney General Mark Earley testified before the US Congress in July 2002 that "anywhere from 250,000 to 600,000" of America's 2.1 million prisoners were forced to have sex against their will each year. The result is an HIV infection rate of 8.5% in New York state's correctional system, which tests its convict population more systematically than others. By comparison, the estimated infection rate for the civilian US population is 0.3%.

What is especially tragic is that those 250,000 to 600,000 inmate rape victims include the overwhelming majority of the 14,500 juvenile boys and girls held in adult jails and prisons. Because they are familiar with the criminal justice system, prosecutors know full well that they are in effect imposing capital-punishment-by-virus whenever they put a juvenile on trial as an adult. But failure to do so would mean losing their next election, so the gruesome practice of providing hardened convicts with underage sex toys continues.

Rape is no less traumatic for adult inmates, however. Just being sexually assaulted *without* being raped in 1991 affected me deeply for years—and I was incredibly, almost freakishly lucky. Whoever is weak is a likely victim: especially the many mentally ill prisoners, the young and the non-gang affiliated. Often these men are reduced to becoming prostitutes in order to channel or contain the crowds of suitors who swarm in after the first "breaking-in." In one case I still recall many years later, a burglar in his mid-twenties took to calling himself Baby-doll and charged $1.09 for oral sex (a pack of Doral cigarettes at 87 cents and two packs of iced tea mix for 11 cents each). That did not take the pressure off him, however: his cellmate eventually held him hostage in their cell and sold him to his associates, who "pulled trains" on him. Of course the guards did not intervene; after years of working in prison, correctional officers often grow calluses on their souls and find it more convenient to do nothing.

How anyone subjected to that kind of experience—and infected with HIV/AIDS to boot—is supposed to put together a reasonably normal life after leaving prison is beyond my imagination. That is why inmate rape is the second of my two fundamental objections to rehabilitation behind bars. No amount of remedial reading classes or anger control courses or drug therapy can possibly outweigh the harm caused to 250,000 to 600,000 prisoners each year by their fellow convicts. Quite apart from the heartwarming tales of reformed inmates, there are plenty of "hard heads" in the penitentiary who may or may not eventually be rehabilitated—but who, in the meantime, destroy the lives of those prisoners who are "soft" enough to change.

"*L'enfer, c'est les autres,*" wrote Jean-Paul Sartre in *No Exit*: "Hell is other people." That is never more true than in prison, and that is why rehabilitation behind bars does not work.

MYTH NO. 5:

There are no alternatives to prison.

So far in the pages of this essay, I have compared the penal policies of this country negatively with those of my own and other industrialized nations. Now we will focus on some of the many instances of local and state governments in America pursuing wise and effective new approaches to crime and prison. Unfortunately, these initiatives are often shamefully underfunded, very small in scale, or not coordinated with complementary efforts in the same and neighboring jurisdictions. By describing some of these successful substitutes to prison from around the country, I hope to encourage a redirection of scarce public funds into programs that not only reduce crime more effectively, but also cost significantly less than incarceration.

But before we examine such alternatives, I want to state emphatically that I believe penitentiaries to be necessary and useful institutions. I have eighteen years behind bars, so I know better than you ever will that there are plenty of men (and presumably women) in prison who should remain there. Perhaps one day they too will see the light and change—but until they do, they need to stay in "the big house" a while longer.

What we will attempt to determine below is whether

there are certain categories of criminals who are currently being sent to jail, but who could be handled differently by the courts. If so, then these men and women need not burden taxpayers by taking up residence in a penitentiary. They could, for instance, be sentenced to community supervision.

Community Supervision

North Carolina put this theory into practice as long ago as 1994, when its legislature reformed sentencing laws. Immediately, the rate of incarceration after arrest fell from 42% to 20%, with enormous savings: whereas each prisoner costs the state $23,800 per year, probation or parole expenses range from $668 per year for regular supervision to $4,187 for the strictest level of enforcement. In the first year that home monitoring by electronic bracelet was introduced in Florida, that state saved the equivalent of 7.5 penitentiaries in operating costs. Only 16% of participants violated the conditions of their home confinement, and just 27% recidivated later—less than half the rate for prison.

Criminal Justice Theory

The question is, precisely which offenders should be eligible for alternatives to jail, such as community supervision? This is essentially a moral determination which, at least in classic jurisprudential theory, hangs on the balance between the relative seriousness of the crime, the level of responsibility of the perpetrator, and the needs of society as a whole. Under this model, the level of punishment is determined by:

- the victim's desire to see the crime punished and, wherever possible, to obtain restitution;

> "Currently, we spend next to nothing on community-based corrections. We get what we pay for."
>
> **John J. Dilulio Jr.**, "Two Million Prisoners Are Enough,"
> *Wall Street Journal*, March 12, 1999

- the offender's *mens rea*, or criminal intent—that is, the degree to which his or her ability to freely choose to break the law was impaired by the factors we discussed in Myth No. 2 (mental illness, the influence of drugs or alcohol, lack of education, low IQ and youth); and
- the community's need on the one hand to uphold respect for the law, and on the other to convert an expensive liability (an incarcerated criminal) into a productive asset (a tax-paying citizen).

The United States has largely abandoned this approach over the last thirty years, however, thanks to a number of extremely high-profile crimes such as John Hinckley Jr.'s assassination attempt on President Ronald Reagan in 1981 and the abduction-murder of Polly Klaas in California in 1993. Since all of us tend to sympathize with victims—especially with likeable ones like the president and a tragic little girl—it feels right and natural to view any crime only from the perspective of those who have been hurt. The harshest possible penalty for the offender seems barely enough; we want him or her to feel all of our pain *and* just a little extra.

I, too, have felt the tug of this powerful need for righteous vengeance, at the very least in the case of the convict who attempted to rape me in 1991. Chemical castration?

Too easy! But when a modern industrialized nation bases its entire court and legal system on this essentially emotional approach to justice, the result is a prison system with 2.1 million inmates that continues to expand even as crime rates drop.

Perhaps the time has come for the citizens of this country to engage in a rational discussion of the issues involved. Although it *feels* good, is it really wise or just or affordable to impose a forty-five-year adult prison sentence on a seventeen-year-old burglar, as in the case of a friend of mine? Or should the judge have considered his *mens rea*: he was diagnosed with a severe case of ADHD (Attention Deficit and Hyperactivity Disorder), on drugs at the time of the burglary, lacked more than a seventh-grade education due to his dyslexia, and was as hormonally impaired as any other seventeen-year-old? And should the judge have pondered how many children will not get new schoolbooks because this one individual has already cost the state roughly half a million dollars to house in jail—with at least another decade's worth of incarceration costs to come?

Drug Offenders

In California, voters have not only begun the public discussion of such questions, but they have already taken direct action to change at least one part of that state's legal system through the referendum process. After the passage of Proposition 36 in 2002, 30,468 drug offenders were sent to treatment instead of to jail in the first year alone—a massive shift away from prison, given California's total correctional population of just over 160,000. Nine other states have at least reduced drug penalties because "at some point, you're going to run out of money," according to Connecticut State Representative Michael Lawler.

Diverting drug offenders from prison to treatment is projected to save California $250 million over four years.

And that limited money is simply more effective when invested in treatment. California's state government has found that every dollar spent on substance abuse therapy generates seven dollars in savings through reduced crime and hospitalization. The RAND Corporation calculates that $1 million invested in longer prison sentences would reduce the consumption of drugs by 13 kilograms; the same $1 million spent on arresting more dealers would lower consumption by 27 kilograms; and investing those $1 million in treatment would reduce consumption by 100 kilograms. In a poll of chiefs of police from around America, 59% expressed a belief that court-supervised treatment is more effective than sending offenders to prison or jail.

But initiatives like California's Proposition 36 only affect new non-violent drug-offenders; those sentenced to sometimes very long terms of incarceration in the past remain behind bars.

How many men and women now serving time would never have seen the inside of a penitentiary if they had been sentenced under Proposition 36? Even according to the most conservative estimates, "at least a quarter" of all inmates, or 525,000 nationwide. And what should be done with them? Simply "RELEASE drug-only offenders," counsels criminologist John J. DiIulio Jr., of "super-predator" fame—so long as they then get therapy in the community.

Instituting measures like Proposition 36 in all fifty states, making such laws retroactive, and funding enough treatment centers for all current and past offenders would be a significant and, above all, politically realistic start to reforming this country's correctional systems. According to an ABC News poll, 75% of Americans already agree, without needing further persuasion, that first- and even second-time drug-offenders should be sentenced to therapeutic programs instead of jail. But non-violent substance abusers are only one of several large sub-groups of criminals whom a better-informed public may not wish to see incarcerated.

The Mentally Ill

Earlier we noted that 20% of all inmates are so obviously deranged that even prison medical departments must officially acknowledge their mental illness. In virtually all penitentiaries, these men and women are simply mixed in with the general population, where they are financially and sexually exploited by other convicts. This lack of care has, however, given me the opportunity to come to know a great many mentally ill inmates during the eighteen years of my incarceration. So I can attest from extensive personal experience that most, perhaps all of these unfortunate people do indeed require some form of institutionalization—but that this institutionalization should never take place in a penitentiary setting.

When I go to my current prison's weight room, I sometimes end up working out with an inmate from this facility's special Mental Health Unit—an exceedingly unusual community therapeutic program. Pound for pound, this man is one of the strongest individuals I have ever met, and the truth is that he frightens me: his mood changes unpredictably, and he is just too loud. But for some reason he feels relatively comfortable around me and thus seems to seek me out.

What I have begun to intuit from our occasional iron-pumping sessions together is that this man is at least as scared as I am, because he does not understand the world around him. Just about everyone reacts to his illness with fear and hostility, so he in turn responds with aggressive displays and sometimes violent acts. His life must be terribly lonely, and I am ashamed that I lack enough compassion to befriend him.

In my entirely untrained opinion, this man cannot safely be released into society. Nor can the other mentally ill inmates simply be freed, even though most of them are passive and non-violent. The fact is that they barely manage to negotiate everyday life inside a penitentiary, where at least they have guards who order them to shower once a week and medical staff who ensure that they stay on their psychotropic medications. On the other side of the fence, with no one to look after them, they would soon get in trouble with the law again.

Unsupervised de-institutionalization is what led to their incarceration in the first place. In the 1970s and '80s, large mental hospitals around the country were closed under the theory that patients would be provided "care in the community." That never materialized, so "prisons have really become, in many ways, the de facto mental hospitals," according to former correctional psychologist Thomas Fagan, PhD. Only 80,000 patients are still housed in major psychiatric facilities, while roughly 444,000 certified, diagnosed mentally ill men and women are doing time behind bars.

Yet there is now an "enormous, unusual agreement

among police, prison officials, judges, prosecutors and human rights lawyers that something has gone painfully awry with the criminal justice system," the co-author of a 2003 Human Rights Watch report on mentally ill prisoners told the *New York Times*. And there are hopeful signs of change. In 2001, Representatives Ted Strickland (D-OH) and Mike DeWine (R-OH, now a senator) joined with Senators Pete Domenici (R-NM) and the late Paul Wellstone (D-MN) to pass some funding for the creation of mental health courts, comparable to the drug courts already in successful operation around the country. In exchange for a guilty plea, offenders are sentenced to treatment instead of prison, an approach that has lowered recidivism rates in California's drug courts by 77 to 85%. So perhaps there is some hope that the mass incarceration of the mentally ill can in time be reversed.

Insanity Defense

Initiatives like mental health courts will not help my mentally ill weightlifting partner, however. For that, a reform of the insanity defense will be necessary.

Until the assassination attempt on President Ronald Reagan in 1981, most US states and the federal government had been moving toward the adoption of the so-called Durham Rule, by which defendants were found to be only partially responsible for their crimes if their actions were the product of mental illness. But John Hinckley Jr.'s acquittal by reason of insanity resulted in a populist legislative backlash: a return to the so-called McNaughten Rule, which defined insanity as the inability to distinguish right from wrong. By this much stricter standard, defendants who are clearly and flagrantly mentally ill *from a psychiatric point of view* are nevertheless found to be sane *from a legal perspective*—with the result that they are sent to prison instead of a mental hospital. Some are even executed, like Ricky Ray Rector, who asked guards to save the dessert from his last meal so he could eat it the next day.

Unfortunately, such sad spectacles are likely to continue so long as politicians pander to their voters' basest instincts. Just weeks before the 1992 New Hampshire primaries, candidate Bill Clinton returned to his governor's post in Arkansas specifically to be seen presiding over Rector's execution. An alternative approach might have been to educate the public that the McNaughten Rule was defined in England in 1844, long before psychology and psychiatry even became sciences, and that one of Judge McNaughten's original purposes was to *reduce* the use of the death penalty.

One might also have pointed out that the courts of every single other industrialized country assess legal responsibility by some equivalent of the Durham Rule, which takes into account medical progress since 1844. By this definition, English courts today arrive at the verdict of "manslaughter by reason of diminished responsibility," for instance: a mentally ill defendant is judged guilty of committing the act, but since he or she lacked the *mens rea* (or criminal intent) necessary for murder, he or she is sent to a secure psychiatric facility. I observed some of my fellow prisoners undergo precisely this legal process during the more than three years I spent in English jails in the late 1980s, and as far as I could tell, there was no post-verdict rioting in the streets by bloodthirsty Englishmen who insisted on seeing a good hanging.

Perhaps one day American politicians will trust voters' common sense and humanity enough to bring insanity laws at least into the twentieth, let alone the twenty-first century. In the meantime, however, this country's leaders could begin by moving all 440,000 current mentally ill prisoners to low- and medium-security jails set aside for them; transferring the authority for these facilities from correctional departments to public health departments; re-training guards to be psychiatric nurse-helpers; and giving inmate-patients as much freedom as possible within these secure mental hospitals to an extent compatible with their level of illness. All of that might or might not save money overall, through elimination of security measures and reductions in staff levels (e.g., manned gun towers). But the savings in human misery would certainly be enormous.

Juvenile Offenders

Another whole category of inmates who, like the mentally ill, may indeed require some form of institutionalization, but should never be housed in adult prisons, are juvenile offenders. Earlier, we saw that there are today 14,500 such unfortunate boys and girls serving time with hardened convicts, who inevitably prey on these children. In the rest of the civilized world, such practices are quite literally unimaginable; I have had difficulties persuading European friends that I am telling them the truth about this subject.

Germany's criminal justice system, by contrast, gives judges the option of transferring an adult defendant aged eighteen to twenty-one *back to juvenile jurisdiction*, if the accused's emotional development indicates diminished responsibility. And it usually does: according to recent studies by the National Institute for Mental Health, Harvard and UCLA, those areas of the brain that control impulsive behavior and the ability to anticipate consequences undergo massive changes in late adolescence and do not fully mature until a person is in his or early twenties. If memory serves me correctly, I barely had the *mens rea* to cook myself breakfast at age eighteen and nineteen, never mind age sixteen or seventeen—and I do not believe I was unusual in this regard.

Yet as recently as the 2002/2003 session, the US Supreme Court embarrassed this country by once again endorsing the execution of defendants who were juveniles at the time of their crimes. Twenty-one such court-ordered child murders have been carried out in this country since 1976. Since 2001, no other nation in the world has executed a defendant who was under age eighteen during the commission of his or her offense, and only two other countries even provide this option under their laws: Pakistan and the Republic of Congo.

What is so utterly repugnant about this medieval custom of US courts is that therapists know how to successfully rehabilitate even the worst of teenaged criminals. In a May 2001 meta-analysis of four hundred studies on crime reduction programs, the Washington State Institute for Public Policy found that, compared to a current cost of $64,000 per juvenile offender for conventional psychosocial services:

- the Functional Family Therapy program saved $14,149 per child per year and reduced recidivism rates by 30%;
- Multidimensional Treatment Foster Care saved $21,836 and resulted in 60% fewer days incarceration; and
- Multisystemic Therapy saved $31,661 with 25 to 70% lower long-term re-arrest rates.

"We've come a long way from a few years ago when the claim was 'nothing works,' " according to John Williams, acting deputy chief of the federal Office of Juvenile Justice and Delinquency Prevention.

Technical Violators

If youthful offenders should not be housed in adult penitentiaries for primarily moral reasons, then purely practical considerations argue for keeping so-called technical violators of parole and probations conditions out of jail. Earlier we saw that, of the 625,000 inmates released from correctional departments across the country each year, 158,750 ex-cons return to the penitentiary within three years for committing new crimes, while 165,000 come back only for violating post-release rules like "failure to follow required instructions." Thanks to this policy, technical violators now constitute more than 27,000 of California's 160,000 inmates; at a cost of $26,000 per California convict per year, that amounts to a $700 million annual bill for incarcerating *non-felons* in one state alone. Yet ratcheting up the intensity of management by parole and probation officers would cost at most one sixth as much, as we found in our discussion of community supervison.

Over-sentencing

Finally, the jail and prison population of the United States could be further reduced by addressing the interrelated problems of over-sentencing and older and geriatric inmates. In many ways, over-sentenced and elderly convicts are the least sympathetic class of prisoners we will examine here and thus politically the most difficult to release. But it is precisely this category of jailbirds that costs the most to house, yet reduces crime the least.

Ever-longer prison sentences are one of the two major reasons why the US correctional population has expanded so dramatically in the last twenty to thirty years. "From the mid-1980s to the early 1990s, prison growth was driven most forcefully by the war on drugs," according to a new study. But "in the 1990s, the primary cause of prison growth . . . became longer sentences rather than more prison admissions."

Longer prison sentences also account for much of the difference in rates of incarceration between the US and other industrialized countries. While those nations catch and convict criminals at rates similar to America's, their courts uniformly impose much shorter terms of confinement. A Canadian burglar serves on average one third as much time as his US counterpart, and a British robber only one half.

So why is there no mayhem in Montreal and London, with all those felons back on the streets so soon? Because crime is essentially a young man's game; there is simply no need to keep perpetrators locked up once they are out of their crime-prone years.

Actuarial tables for arrest rates by age make fascinating reading in this regard. For robbery, the peak ages are sixteen through eighteen; for burglary, fifteen through eighteen; and for aggravated assault, seventeen through twenty-one. Thirty-five- to forty-year-olds, on the other hand, rob and burgle at one fifth the rate of teenagers and commit assault less than half as often. By age forty-five to fifty, the rates for robbery and burglary approach zero, while the rate for aggravated assault is less than a quarter of the teen spike. "Most men age out of committing violent crimes in their thirties," notes New York City Corrections Commissioner Michael Jacobson. "It is difficult to say you are preventing crime by locking up men in their fifties, sixties and seventies."

According to the Bureau of Justice Statistics, ex-cons forty-five and older re-offend at a rate 41% lower than eighteen- to twenty-four-year-olds. Of those fifty-five and

> "I have since come to realize that the provisions of the [mandatory minimum sentencing] law have led to terrible injustices and that signing it was a mistake—an overly punishing and cruel response that gave no discretion to a sentencing judge, even for extenuating circumstances."
>
> **Former Michigan Governor William G. Milliken**, who originally signed that state's mandatory minimum sentencing measure into law, *Detroit News*, September 20, 2002

over, only 1.4% break the law again after leaving prison. The "over the hill gang" is a Hollywood fantasy, not a criminological reality.

Elderly Inmates and "Three Strikes"

There are more and more elderly inmates filling this country's prisons, however: today's figure of 125,000 is expected to rise to *one third* of the total correctional population by 2030. Due to higher medical expenses, incarcerating an older prisoner costs three times as much as a younger one, so that by 2020 health care expenses for elderly convicts in California will amount to $5 *billion*—the entire prison budget for 2002. Yet talk of releasing these graying felons is anathema to men like Michael Pickett, a deputy director of California's prison department: he claims to have seen "inmates in wheelchairs 'beat the bark off men standing on their own two feet.' "

No doubt Mr. Pickett is also an ardent defender of California's "three strikes" law, a major reason why that

Arrest Rates by Age

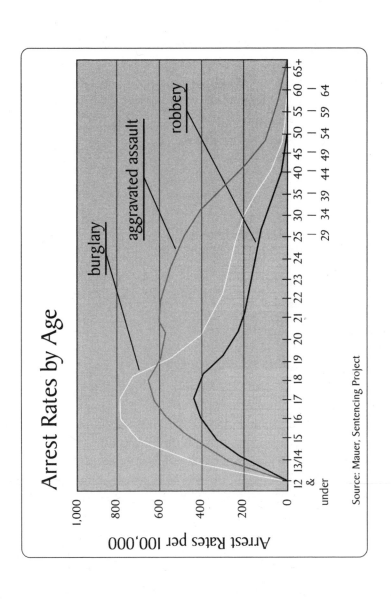

Source: Mauer, Sentencing Project

state houses so many elderly prisoners. As recently as 2003, the US Supreme Court ruled that these laws are not cruel and unusual, even if the third "strike" is only for the theft of $68.64 worth of videotapes. But while a life sentence (!) for petty theft may pass constitutional muster in the Rehnquist Court, we can still inquire whether such practices make fiscal sense. The thief in that 2003 Supreme Court case would have to steal $71.23 worth of videotapes every single day of the year, including weekends and holidays, to justify the $26,000 annual cost of incarceration in California.

Could the "three strikes" law be cruel and unusual for taxpayers, if not for criminals?

Honor Building

In the penitentiary where I am currently housed, I live in a building full of the sort of vicious geriatrics Mr. Pickett fears, the kind who can "beat the bark off" relative youngsters like me. This is the so-called honor building, for long-term prisoners who have not committed a rules infraction in many years. Virtually all of these convicts have served upwards of twenty-five years behind bars and are now between forty-five and seventy years old. Around here, I am considered "fresh meat," a "new fish" with just eighteen years under my belt.

Without these "honor" inmates, this prison—and, indeed, all penitentiaries anywhere—would collapse immediately. We are the foremen at the chair factory, the chief cooks, the plumbers and electricians and locksmiths (yes!), the senior teacher's aides, the housing unit clerks, and the department heads' secretaries. While our civilian or uniformed "supervisors" play video games on the new computers the Department of Corrections has placed in every sergeant's office, we do most of the work, fill out the endless DOC forms, and solve most problems before staff members even notice them. And, yes, just like in the movies, we occasionally advise guards on income tax matters, retirement packages and workers' compensation claims.

So convinced is the administration of our utter dependability that there are often no guards at all posted on the floors of the honor building, and neither cell nor wing doors are locked all night long. As far as I know, there has been no case of cell-burglary in years; in fact, not even loud talking in the hallways is tolerated by convicts trying to rest up for work the next day. Enforcing both written and unwritten rules on each other is so popular in the honor building that the guards do not even have to pay their snitches here, as they do in other buildings.

As a result, the social atmosphere in the honor building is downright pleasant, even if the amenities are spartan. A Vietnam veteran in his fifties recently organized a geriatric exercise class for inmates in their sixties who have suffered strokes or are awaiting spinal surgery. On weekends, gray-haired "old heads" sit in the dayroom and reminisce about the last time they saw their hometowns, "back in the day" when Gerald Ford was President. If we only had shuffle-board, this could be Florida.

No Parole: A Hidden Form of Capital Punishment

Many of these men are technically still eligible for parole, including that friend of mine whom I mentioned earlier: at sixteen and seventeen, he smoked methamphetamines and burgled neighbors' houses in his wealthy white subdivision; at eighteen, he was sentenced to forty-five years behind bars; today he is forty-one and works as a clerk in this penitentiary's Mental Health Unit, an especially trusted position; and in another ten or twelve years, he may actually go home. His misfortune was to have been sentenced before the abolition of parole, when defendants were expected to serve only one fourth or one third of the "official" prison term imposed.

But now that new inmates are no longer eligible for any form of earned early release, correctional departments have also stopped granting so-called "discretionary parole" to convicts who at least theoretically could be freed and in the past certainly would have been paroled. "We assume that the judge did not intend for them to be released when they were sixty-five," said Virginia's parole board chairperson Helen Fahey to explain why such very long-term inmates are not being released even under Virginia's geriatric parole statute. The contrary is true, however: judges imposing sentences fifteen or twenty years ago, before the abolition of parole, never imagined that the criminals they were sending to jail would be in effect detained until death.

What this policy amounts to is a hidden form of capital punishment for the 127,677 inmates in this country's state and federal prisons who are serving life sentences. According to a recent study by the Sentencing Project, one out of every eleven penitentiary inmates is a lifer, an 83% rise since 1992. The federal system and six states do not parole prisoners with life sentences at all, and virtually all the others do so only rarely.

Of California's 160,000 inmates, for example, an astonishing 25,000, or 15.6%, are serving life sentences. Only five of these lifers had their §3041(a) parole date grants approved for release by Governor Gray Davis between 1999 and 2003; the rest must expect never to leave prison.

As one of many who face this fate in Virginia, I can assure you that a life sentence without any hope of freedom feels like a death sentence. Conversations about suicide are commonplace among my associates. And in the not-too-distant future—once we can no longer avoid facing the truth—many of us will stop talking, I predict.

Reintegration

With some help, however, it turns out that very long-term inmates will hardly re-offend at all upon release. Ironically enough, this is especially true of those who have served long terms for homicide; released murderers consistently have the lowest recidivism rates of *any* group of offenders. Though the public never hears of them, many programs for reintegrating prisoners have decades-long track records of success:

- George Washington University's POPS Program has worked individually with older long-term inmates in five states since 1989 without a single act of recidivism on the part of those released.
- In Detroit, the Prison Fellowship Ministries TOP Program has achieved re-offense rates of only 1%, even though it focuses on high-risk ex-convicts. The secret to its success is to have a church "adopt" a released felon, thus providing him with a caring support network that assists him in becoming a productive citizen—perhaps for the first time.
- Brooklyn's District Attorney Charles "Joe" Hynes used his department's funds to hire a full-time social worker who assists parolees and probationers in finding legal

employment, lowering the recidivism rate of participants by 60%.

- Founded by two Catholic priests in 1972, Chicago's Safer Foundation now helps 5,000 released prisoners annually in securing jobs and substance abuse treatment. Even its most intensive and expensive facility, the Adult Transition Center for inmates on work release, costs $2,000 less per year than incarceration.

- San Francisco's Delancey Street Restaurant has been a Bay Area landmark for over thirty years. Not many diners realize, however, that it operates with an all-ex-convict staff under the leadership of Dr. Mimi Silbert, of UC-Berkeley. Over 14,000 former inmates have transitioned through the restaurant back into society.

- Crossover Restorative Ministries of Gordonsville, Virginia, was founded by a former prisoner who now employs other freed jailbirds as construction workers, rebuilding—among other things—a neighbor's house destroyed by fire.

- Even the federal government knows how to integrate prisoners after they return to society, as it proved in its VJO Program with a particularly volatile clientele: violent juvenile offenders. In the Detroit and Boston study groups, skilled case managers helped youths leaving the penitentiary to find jobs and to develop positive social relationships in a "graduated re-entry." This holistic or "ecological" approach lowered recidivism rates significantly, and there is no reason to believe that similarly intense management of the grumpy old men in my honor building would be any less successful.

Of course all of these reintegration initiatives depend on a willingness to *try*—and that cannot always be found in

Departments of Correction. In Virginia, for instance, those long-term inmates most in need of help are not eligible for that state's offender re-entry program, which is reserved only for non-violent criminals. Thus, after serving twenty, thirty and more years, the few "old heads" lucky enough to leave that state's prisons at all are simply put back on the street, to fend for themselves as best they can. Not exactly a recipe for success.

Supreme Court Justice Kennedy

Having spent so many years living in close proximity with these aging felons, I cannot help but sympathize with them, so my special pleading on their behalf should be taken with a grain of salt. Most of them have committed horrible crimes, after all, and they certainly deserved to spend a decade or two behind bars in atonement. But twenty-five years, or thirty? Is that extra vengeance inflicted on them worth the $60,000 to $70,000 per year it costs to house each elderly inmate?

Revenge has been called "the dark pleasure," and like any pleasure it comes at a price. When that price exceeds $50 billion per year, as it does now, it may be time to examine alternatives to "an eye for an eye." "Forgiveness is not just some nebulous, vague idea that one can easily dismiss. It has to do with uniting people through practical politics," said Archbishop Desmond Tutu, chair of South Africa's Truth and Reconciliation Commission. "Without forgiveness, there is no future." For state and federal budgets, we might add, perhaps not even a financial future.

In Europe, life sentences last twenty years, and a proposal of "life without parole" was greeted with "emphatic . . . rejection" by all parties in Britain's House of Commons. While European attitudes in this area are shaped by human rights considerations, the United States may yet come to the same conclusion for budgetary reasons. "Our resources are misspent, our punishments too severe, our sentences too long," US Supreme Court Justice Anthony M. Kennedy told the American Bar Association in a speech on August 10, 2003. He then added that, "in too many cases, [long sentences] are unjust," too.

Five hundred twenty-five thousand non-violent "drug-only" offenders, 440,000 officially diagnosed mentally ill inmates, 14,500 juveniles in adult penitentiaries, 165,000 technical violators who committed no new crime, and at least 125,000 elderly convicts: theoretically, that amounts to 1,269,500 men, women and children who do not belong in jail or prison and should be removed expeditiously from America's overblown correctional departments. But the vast majority of these releasable or transferable inmates fall into two or more of the above categories—elderly addicts, mentally ill technical violators, etc.—so the actual number of convicts "lost" from the penitentiary system will in fact be much lower than the 1.2 million suggested above. With a little luck and number-fudging, the United States may even retain its rank as world leader in incarcerating its own citizens.

How nice.

MYTH NO. 6:

Criminal justice issues are so important that no one would dare mislead the public about them.

After surveying Myths No. 1 through 5, you may be asking yourself: why was I not told any of this before now? Who has been misleading the public about the growing correctional crisis for the last two or three decades? Or are you, the author, deceiving me, the reader?

Allow me to address the last question first by admitting that I, like everyone, have a personal agenda: to free as many of my fellow convicts as possible, since I myself will never be released. While I am technically eligible for parole now, the extremely high profile of my criminal trial—and my continuing refusal to admit guilt—makes it politically impossible to deport me to my home country of Germany. So none of the penological proposals I make in this essay can help me gain my own freedom.

While we are on the issue of my bias, I should make you aware that I have a personal antipathy for former President Bill Clinton, whose criminal justice policies exploited voters' understandable fear of crime, pandered to their basest emotional need for revenge, and greatly accelerated the unwise over-expansion of the prison system in the 1990s.

Any hope for correcting the mistakes of the past comes from:

- religious conservatives like Charles Colson and his Prison Fellowship Ministries, whose InnerChange prison and TOP reintegration programs actually work;
- fiscal conservatives, who may come to recognize mass incarceration as a classic government boondoggle that wastes public treasure and does not effectively control crime; and
- law and order conservatives, who may be persuaded that "tough on crime" can mean less tough on criminals and more tough on the causes of criminal behavior (or, to use their idiom: hate the sin but love the sinner).

Having addressed my bias, we can return to the question with which we began Myth No. 6: why have you not heard until now most of the information I have presented here?

Let me assure you that there is no vast right-wing conspiracy to deny you the truth about America's correctional systems—unless Bill Clinton was a member of the cabal, too. Instead, we have a number of diverse interest groups who are often bitterly at odds with each other, but who nevertheless manage to agree on one thing: the United States needs more penitentiaries! Of course unions prefer public prisons, while industry likes private jails—but those are side issues. Either way, the end result is an ever-increasing number of correctional facilities.

So let us examine the various sources of sometimes unreliable information on criminology and penology to see if we can discover their biases as we discovered mine.

Criminologists and Penologists

Like all people, academic researchers have agendas that are not always clear, but whose distorting effect can skew the conclusions they draw from statistical evidence. The classic example here is the famous "prison pays" argument, according to which the economic damage caused by felons is far higher than the expense of locking them up. When looked at more closely, however, it turns out that this theory depends overwhelmingly not on the value of items stolen, for instance, but on the "cost" of homicides.

And that is where the number-juggling enters: in one study, each murder was assumed to "cost" $3 million, of which $1 million was for lost wages, etc., and almost $2 million was for "loss of quality of life." Of course every homicide is a grave human tragedy—but why use the figure of $2 million? Through the use of arbitrary numbers like this, one researcher determined that the national "cost" of "pain and suffering" from crime was $345 *billion.*

Number-juggling has in the past contributed directly to the unrestrained expansion of America's correctional systems. In the infamous Zedlewski report of 1987, a Department of Justice researcher claimed that incarcerating a single offender saved taxpayers $405,000, a striking figure that candidates from both political parties used in subsequent elections to call for more prisons. Unfortunately, Zedlewski's methodology was so skewed that, using his theory's mathematical model, the first phase of the prison-building boom in the early to mid-1980s should have sufficed to eliminate all crime in the United States completely by 1986—the year *before* he wrote his report.

In a 1994 study, California criminologists "proved" that passing the "three strikes" proposal then pending in the state legislature would prevent 8,000 murders per year. How could any legislator vote against saving 8,000 lives? So the "three strikes" proposal became law—even though California only experienced 3,700 murders in the year of the bill's passage!

Unions

Unions, which are usually assumed to be politically left-leaning, did not oppose California's "three strikes" proposal by pointing out the underlying study's sheer illogic, for the simple reason that one of that state's most powerful unions—the California Correctional Peace Officers Association (CCPOA), or guards' union—supported its passage with $101,000 of its members' dues. In fact, the CCPOA is the single largest contributor to California political campaigns, spending $2 million to elect Gray Davis to the governorship in 1998. Just two months after his campaign committee received a $251,000 check from the CCPOA in 2002, Governor Davis signed a new labor agreement with the union that assured guards a 34% pay increase over five years.

Over half a million Americans now work in this country's jails and penitentiaries, more than for any Fortune 500 company save General Motors. And, quite understandably, all those guards and counselors and correctional educators and nurses react very sharply if their livelihoods are threatened by penal reform proposals. When New Jersey's Corrections Commissioner Devon Brown came out in support of revising that state's sentencing laws, for instance, a prison guards' union accused him of "implement[ing] a policy to return violent criminals to all of our neighborhoods simply to save money." That did not get their boss fired, so the union next charged him with "aggravat[ing] tensions between inmates and corrections officers" by giving a speech at a conference on minorities in prison. At last report, Commissioner Brown had not been dismissed *yet*—but Governor James E. McGreevey's spokesperson was forced to publicly reassure the guards union that "the governor does not support the early release of prisoners." Sometimes "tough on crime" is just another way of saying "jobs for the boys."

Industry

For industry, "law and order" slogans are advertising for private prison companies like Wackenhut or Corrections Corporation of America, as one of the industry's own investment solicitation letters makes clear: "While arrests and convictions are steadily on the rise, profits are to be made—profits from crime. Get in on the ground floor of this booming industry now." Those profits are made by paying guards in private prisons substantially lower wages, with predictable results: a 41% staff turnover rate, versus 15% in public penitentiaries, and up to 190% more "serious incidents" within corporate-owned prisons than in state-owned correctional facilities. In 2001, 142,521 adult Americans were incarcerated in private jails and penitentiaries, and the value of the industry as a whole was estimated to be $2 billion.

Even when corporations do not own and operate prisons, there are plenty of revenue-generating opportunities behind bars. The Aramark Corporation, for instance, expects to make a $58 million profit per year by feeding convicts in the Florida Department of Corrections for only $2.32 per man per day. Yet its contract with the Ohio Department of Corrections was not renewed because of "inexcusable" sanitation problems and "a near riot during

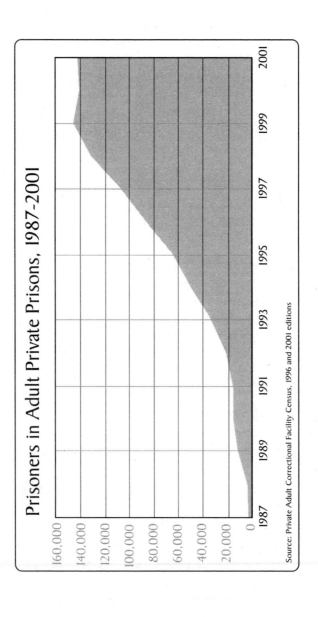

Prisoners in Adult Private Prisons, 1987–2001

160,000
140,000
120,000
100,000
80,000
60,000
40,000
20,000
0

1987   1989   1991   1993   1995   1997   1999   2001

Source: Private Adult Correctional Facility Census, 1996 and 2001 editions

> "Incarceration is a prosperous industry, and one with a glowing future—as is true of all the others linked to the great hiding away of the American poor."
>
> **Loïc Wacquant**, *Les prisons de la misère*

breakfast as a result of (Aramark's) strict compliance with portion size(s)," according to an Ohio DOC inspection team. For MCI, penitentiary payphones are the big money-makers: each prison phone generates $15,000 income per year, compared to only $3,000 for the average payphone in the "free world."

In Virginia, MCI pays the Department of Corrections a 60% commission on revenues from inmate phone calls—an extra $6 to $8 million per year that the nearly insolvent state sorely needs. Both the telecommunications company and the government seek to maximize their profits under this deal: while federal convicts pay $3 for a fifteen-minute call, Virginia state prisoners are charged up to $9.20 for the same fifteen minutes. This price-gouging was declared illegal by the State Corporation Commission in 2001—whereupon the Virginia legislature passed a special bill removing such matters from the SCC's authority. Curiously enough, the sponsor of that measure, state Senator Thomas K. Norment Jr. (R-Williamsburg), had just received the third-largest campaign contribution of the previous election cycle . . . from MCI!

Naphcare's model for business success is to provide medical services to prisons at lower cost than state-employed penitentiary nurses. In Alabama, that means housing all of the state's HIV/AIDS-infected inmates in a single converted warehouse "infested with spiders, rats and birds," according to a recently filed lawsuit. Although the Department of Justice found that the AIDS-related death rate of Alabama convicts was twice the national average for prisoners, Naphcare's spokesperson maintained that the company "provides quality, compassionate care to Alabama inmates." What really matters is, of course, that the profit margin stays healthy.

Understandably, Aramark, MCI, Naphcare and the others are interested in maintaining their captive consumer base. One way they do this is through the American Legislative Exchange Council (ALEC), a private industry lobbying group that drafts statutes friendly to business and then pushes those laws through state legislatures. When companies no longer wanted to bear legal responsibility for cleaning up their own pollution, for instance, ALEC created a model bill called "Environmental Audit Privilege," versions of which were passed in at least three states.

Corrections Corporation of America was a member of the task force that drafted ALEC's "truth in sentencing" statute, ultimately enacted in forty states. These measures greatly restricted parole eligibility and thus increased the number of prisoners—to the direct benefit of Corrections Corporation of America. Yet "there was never any mention that ALEC or anybody else had any involvement in this," said Walter Dickey, the former head of Wisconsin's correctional department after his state passed a version of the measure submitted by ALEC members.

In this case, at least, "truth in sentencing" might have been more appropriately called "truth in advertising"—for Corrections Corporation of America, that is.

Local Politicians

Nor can local politicians be trusted to tell voters the full truth about the long-term consequences of the prison-building boom. With farming, mining and logging in structural decline, penitentiaries are increasingly becoming the primary employers in small towns like Ionia, Michigan, home to six correctional facilities with 5,094 convicts and 1,584 guards. A full 60% of prisons are now built in rural counties as local leaders compete for these secure, though low-paying jobs.

According to the author of a new Urban Institute study on expanding correctional systems, "we've seen the development of a prison construction advocacy position" by politicians hoping for new taxpayer "money for community health services, roads and local law enforcement." Nearly a third of all counties in those states studied now have at least one jail or penitentiary, thanks to energetic lobbying by lawmakers. Thus "the prison network is now deeply intertwined with American life, deeply integrated into the physical and economic infrastructure of a large number of American counties," the Institute concludes.

But penitentiary politics do not end there. As a matter of law, the US Census Bureau considers convicts to be residents *in their prisons*, not in their homes. Thus 6.99% of the "residents" of New York State Redistricting Taskforce member Chris Ortloff's new rural district are, in fact, penitentiary inmates, while Sussex County, Virginia, was declared the fastest growing county in the US in the late 1990s because two new supermax prisons increased its "population" by 23%. When it comes to appropriating both state and federal funds, all those new "residents" bring home much-needed pork for rural districts—between

$5 and $8 million for the lucky hosts of Wisconsin's transferred convicts, for example.

Federal Government

Even the federal government cannot be trusted entirely on some of the further-reaching effects of mass incarceration. Of course we already know that the official mid-2003 unemployment rate of 6% is at best a half-truth: the figure of 8.8 million officially unemployed includes neither the 4.8 million part-time workers seeking but unable to find full-time jobs, nor the 1.4 million people who looked for work within the last year but meanwhile gave up and dropped out of the labor market altogether. What is often overlooked, however, is that American unemployment figures also do not take into account the 2.1 million adult inmates of jails and prisons.

If the US incarcerated its own citizens at Western European rates—or the American rate of the 1970s—only 300,000 men and women would be behind bars in this country instead of 2.1 million. This nation's "excess" 1.8 million convicts should, therefore, be counted as unemployed to make a comparison fair and balanced. Doing so would raise the American unemployment rates to 7.2%, however—right in line with the allegedly underperforming "socialist" Western European economies.

Could it be that the US government is keeping its unemployment rates artificially low by locking up unneeded workers? Perhaps that is not the intent, but it is certainly the effect. If 1.8 million unskilled ex-convict job-seekers were to suddenly flood onto the labor market, the macroeconomic effects would be devastating. Better not to even think of that possibility. And, therefore, better not to mention any alternatives to mass incarceration.

> If those incarcerated were counted, the overall unemployment rate for black men would increase by about two thirds.

Departments of Correction

Prison systems are understandably secretive, since caging human beings is inevitably a nasty business. And the Virginia Department of Corrections is no different: another inmate-author, Joseph Giarratano, was transferred all the way to Utah in the 1990s. Unfortunately, I can expect to be moved to some suitably oppressive new penitentiary as punishment for what you are reading, too.

Most instances of correctional obfuscation are not that obvious, of course. An excellent case study in this regard is how prison systems deal with contagious diseases, such as the outbreak of drug-resistant tuberculosis in New York's jails and prisons in 1989. Through guards and hospitalized inmates, this airborne pathogen was spread to civilians in the community, leading to hundreds of deaths in the metropolitan area and a $1 billion containment effort. This horrific episode persuaded the New York Department of Correctional Services to test its inmate population more systematically for contagious diseases than other states' prison systems. And that gives us an opportunity for some interesting comparisons.

According to the Bureau of Justice Statistics, 2.2% of state and 0.8% of federal convicts are infected with the HIV/AIDS virus, and the Virginia Department of Corrections gives a figure of just under 2%. Those rates are high, compared to a civilian US rate of 0.3%, but not shockingly so. When we turn to the New York prison system, however, we find that 8.5% of inmates there are infected with HIV/AIDS. Why so large a difference?

Either convicts in New York jails simply have much more unhealthy lifestyles than prisoners in other states (something I can definitely deny) or New York correctional medical services do more testing than other states' penitentiary nurses (something I can definitely confirm). Only twenty states bother to test all of their prisoners for HIV, and in Virginia, inmates actually have to pay for their own HIV/AIDS and Hepatitis C tests. Or, to be perfectly accurate: the tests themselves are free, but in order to get them, convicts have to see the doctor first. And that means a $5 "co-payment" charge, or roughly five days' worth of inmate wages at the starting salary of 23 cents an hour.

Not surprisingly, only very few prisoners request tests under those circumstances. That keeps the HIV/AIDS statistics pleasantly low and, more importantly, avoids the necessity of paying for the treatment of inmates known to be infected.

In its "Recommendations and Reports," the Centers for Disease Control does not even bother to call for the full testing of prisoners for the Hepatitis C (HCV) virus, because they know that states are unwilling to accept the financial burden of treating literally hundreds of thousands of infected inmates if their illnesses are officially diagnosed. Between 16 and 41% of America's incarcerated population carries the HCV virus, with annual treatment costs of $15,000 to $25,000. But, according to a recent investigative study, "only fifty inmates out of an estimated 12,800 infected inmates" even receive treatment in Virginia, for instance. "Correctional systems have buried their heads in the sand because they don't want to know how many prisoners have Hepatitis C," says Eric Blaban, staff attorney with the National Prison Project.

What you don't know can't cost you.

The Media

Unfortunately, the American media are no more a source of accurate information about criminological issues than departments of correction. In fact, the lack of balanced reporting has contributed significantly to the propagation of the kind of myths we have examined in this essay.

Although index crimes (those tracked by the FBI) fell by 5.1% between 1995 and 1996, 71% of the public thought there was *more* crime in the United States than the year before. Why? Because the number of crime stories in the media bears no relation to the number of crimes: murder reports on network TV news, for instance, rose by 336% from 1990 to 1995, a period in which the actual homicide rate *fell* by 13%. According to former NBC News President Lawrence Grossman, the reason for this phenomenon is simple: money. Crime stories are cheap to produce!

And, of course, they "sell." I remember well how one tabloid newspaper celebrated my own arrest with the announcement that I had danced naked in my victims' blood. No doubt that raised circulation figures nicely.

Unfortunately, much of what passes for journalism about prison issues is no less skewed than that little gem about me. For an article about Virginia's first detention center for civilly committed sexual predators, for instance, the state's leading newspaper could find no better headline than "Predators get amenities"—because inmates there will be allowed to play basketball and watch TV, just as in a normal jail. No mention was made of the fact that all prison basketballs and prison TVs are paid for by convicts

> "Hound him. Hound this predator creep. Hound him into someone else's neighborhood. Then hound him from there. Hound him and hound him and hound him."
>
> **Kate Nelson**, staff writer, *Albuquerque Tribune*, writing about David Siebers, a released sex offender who tried to settle down in Albuquerque, New Mexico. His house was subsequently burned down by local residents.

themselves, through the profits from penitentiary canteens. Nor did the article comment on the bizarre decision to house these men not in regular cells, but in chicken-wire cages erected inside the housing unit. Finally, there was not even a passing reference to the legal and moral controversy surrounding the relatively new practice of confining sex offenders even after their court-imposed terms of incarceration are over; not everyone agrees that this is constitutional, even it if is wise in some cases. But newspaper readers learned only that "predators get amenities"— *horribile dictu!*

Blaming the media for this sensationalistic approach to criminal justice reporting would be entirely wrong, of course; editors are simply giving the public what it wants. The question is: Are you, as a consumer, willing to demand and pay for serious, contextual, well-researched journalism on how prisons spend your $57 billion each year? Or would you rather hear how I danced naked in my victims' blood and then enjoyed my "amenities"?

Reality Check

If our discussion above has led you to despair of ever finding reliable information on criminology and penology, then allow me to give you a brief introductory bibliography:

- Charles Colson's *Justice That Restores*, on the (religious) right, is the sanest and, above all, most hopeful discussion of this complex subject.
- Marc Mauer's *Race to Incarcerate* and *Invisible Punishment*, on the center-left, are balanced collections of some of the best researchers' writings.
- Peter Wagner's *The Prison Index*, offered through the Prison Policy Initiative and the Western Prison Project, is an absolutely indispensable collection of correctional statistics, presented in an interesting and thought-provoking fashion.

Professor Joan Petersilia has also established a reputation as a leading authority in this field.

But perhaps just as important as the armchair approach to criminology is a raw encounter with reality. I have attempted to offer you a little taste of this through the vignettes of prison life woven into this essay. What you really need to do, however, is to become a volunteer at your local jail or penitentiary.

By sacrificing one evening per week to teach remedial reading to convicts, you will quickly develop a context by which to judge mere academic penology and ivory tower criminology. Much of what sounds good—"tough on crime!" "more accountability!"—falls apart quickly when you encounter real prisoners. On the whole, reality is both more hopeful *and* more frightening than all the myths of life behind bars.

CONCLUSION

To wrap up this essay on America's prison crisis, I offer you one piece of bad and three pieces of good news.

The bad news first: in some respects, the problem is actually much worse than I have described above. Throughout these pages, I have given you average figures for adult Americans of both genders and all races. But when those numbers are broken down by race and sex, they become absolutely terrifying.

The United States currently incarcerates 715 out of 100,000 adults. Because women are imprisoned less frequently than men, white males are in fact jailed at a rate of 990 per 100,000. Black men, however, face odds of 6,838 out of 100,000.

Yes: *6,838* out of 100,000. By comparison, South Africa kept only 851 out of 100,000 of its black men caged in the last year of apartheid.

More than one fifth of all African-American men aged thirty to thirty-four either are now or have already been behind bars, and that number is projected to rise. In Washington DC, the capital of "the greatest nation on earth," *half* of all young black men are in jail or on probation or parole.

> Black offenders constituted 21% of prison admissions in 1926, but 50% of prison admissions in 1996.

As law and order fans are so fond of saying: actions must have consequences. Jailing African-American men at such obscenely disproportionate rates must and will have consequences, as well. And since the United States is already committing this crime against humanity even as you read these lines, there is no way to avoid the coming whirlwind.

I speak as a German, a citizen of a country that committed an even greater national sin in recent memory—and was punished most severely for it. So I wish you good luck and the strength to survive what you are brewing up for yourselves in your penitentiaries and inner-city ghettos.

Now to the three pieces of good news, the most encouraging of which is that some of America's policymakers have already begun to address this country's correctional crisis:

- Thanks to the budget crises affecting governments at all levels, twenty-five states have taken measures like eliminating mandatory minimum sentences, restoring parole and/or early release, and diverting non-violent offenders from prison to treatment.
- Some of the leaders instituting these reforms are the very politicians who, decades earlier, had signed into law the overly punitive and ineffective crime control measures whose reversal they now urge: Michigan's former Governor William G. Milliken, former New York state

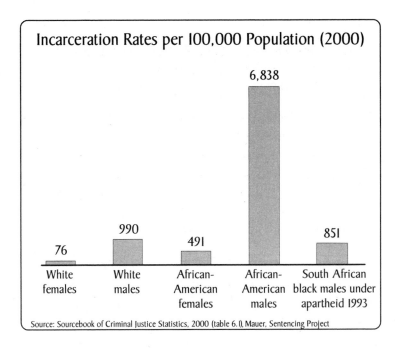

Incarceration Rates per 100,000 Population (2000)

			6,838	
76	990	491		851
White females	White males	African-American females	African-American males	South African black males under apartheid 1993

Source: Sourcebook of Criminal Justice Statistics, 2000 (table 6.1), Mauer, Sentencing Project

Senator John Dunne, and Texas state House Corrections Committee Chairman Ray Allen.

- While other Midwest states experienced increases of nearly 4% in their penitentiary populations between 1998 and 2000, Ohio Governor Bob Taft's reforms resulted in a 6% decline in that state's number of inmates—and a savings of millions of dollars.

- Governor Arnold Schwarzenegger has said he is "gravely concerned" about California's $6 billion per year prison system and wants to reduce its size by revamping the currently moribund parole system. Even better, the California Correctional Peace Officers Association's (CCPOA's) 34% pay increase—granted by a grateful

> "Every white person here and in America [should] take a moment to think how he or she would feel if one in three white men were in similar circumstances."
>
> **President William J. Clinton**, in an October 1995 address on race relations, referring to the fact that one in three African-American men are in jail, on probation, or on parole.

Governor Gray Davis in better days—is likely to be terminated.

Unfortunately, however, not all policymakers have joined this movement toward fiscal prudence and sane penal policies:

- Maryland Governor Robert Ehrlich promised "to get non-violent drug offenders out of jail and into treatment programs" but then enacted the largest prison construction program since the early 1990s.
- Although Virginia, with a population of 7.2 million, has nearly twice as many inmates as Canada, a nation of 30 million, that state proposes to expand its penitentiary system by *another* 30% over the next six years.
- US Attorney General John Ashcroft is stringently enforcing a little-known provision of the USA Patriot Act that places special scrutiny on federal judges who sentence defendants to less than the harsh mandatory minimums prescribed by Congress. As a result of this and other "get tough" measures, the federal Bureau of Prisons is

planning for a 60% increase in its inmate population between 2001 and 2010.

So American taxpayers cannot simply lie back and trust the government to make sufficiently radical changes in this area. As the *Washington Post* noted, "fiscal pressures may indeed *slow the growth* of the vast US prison system. But *reversing the trend* of the past quarter-century is another matter" (italics mine). For that to happen, the citizens of this nation will have to return to their roots, to the tradition of the Minutemen—and take a few direct, individual, personal potshots at the corrections complex.

But why get involved in the prison crisis, when there are so many other issues and causes to support? Why "Free the Felons," when "Save the Whales" is so much more attractive?

Because this country's current addiction to jails and prisons is a betrayal of America's core value: liberty. Once, this was "the land of the free"—but no longer. And that betrayal of the heart of the American dream has moral consequences, as I suggested in the introduction. Every single US citizen who pays taxes directly supports the correctional culture and thus is paying for the slow destruction of his or her own identity as an American. This, I would suggest, is just as urgent as saving the whales.

So, what can *you* do?

This is where my last two pieces of good news come in: one direct-action plan for liberals and another for conservatives. These initiatives could even be implemented together, if left and right will cooperate for once.

First the liberal, "public interest" proposal: force correctional departments to treat *all* inmates infected with HCV and HIV/AIDS. Your rationale would *not* be that prisoners need medical attention—convicts are too unsympathetic for this to succeed—but that the general public must be protected from the spread of lethal diseases through inmates.

Any epidemiologist can confirm that penitentiaries are indeed particularly effective "incubators" for blood-borne pathogens. And 625,000 potential carriers of contagion leave this country's jails and prisons each year—walking viral time bombs.

Because "some prisons have actually cut back on testing for disease, rather than risk being required to treat large numbers of infected inmates at bankrupting costs, . . . released inmates will unknowingly pass on diseases to others," the *New York Times* noted recently. "By failing to confront public health problems in prison, the country could be setting itself up for new epidemics down the line."

Instead of working through legislatures, you would use the court systems in all fifty states to force correctional departments to follow their own health and safety regulations in this regard. Prison systems have a duty to protect the public not only from criminals, but also from medical hazards associated with housing them.

If all infected convicts across the US were treated, the cost nationally would amount to a minimum of $10 billion *per year* ($7.5 billion for HCV and $2.5 billion for HIV/AIDS). The resulting fiscal emergency would be of unprecedented proportions, far beyond anything cash-strapped state budgets face even today. And in that environment, real reforms would suddenly appear . . . *prudent*.

And now the conservative, faith-based proposal, which I

personally find much more appealing: expand Prison Fellowship Ministry's TOP Program nationally.

In 2001, America's 134 mainline Christian denominations had 317,580 houses of worship. If each congregation "adopted" just *two* of the 625,000 inmates released from prison each year, there might only be 6,250 recidivists (at TOP's rate of 1%) instead of 421,875 real and technical violators (at the current national rate of 67.5%). That would starve the correctional monster of the flesh and blood it needs to stay alive.

Suddenly, there would be entire penitentiaries standing empty, bereft of recidivists who failed to recidivate—because they now have jobs, thanks to their new church-based social networks. No doubt prison guards' unions would force lawmakers to stop all forms of early release immediately, for fear of losing their members' jobs. But hardly any convicts are released early anymore, anyway—most have to serve 85 to 90% of their sentences nowadays—so in the second year of this plan's operation, another few hundred thousand inmates would be lost to correctional systems nationwide as they were "adopted" by churches in their hometowns. And yet more penitentiaries would go unneeded.

As unneeded as most of them—though not all—are today.

NOTES

INTRODUCTION

PAGE

1 *"This year, some 600,000"*: Reuters, "Bush Proposal on Ex-Felons Welcomed by Left, Right," *New York Times*, January 21, 2004.

2 *thirty-year low*: Richard Willing, "Crime Rate Hits 30-Year Low," *USA Today*, August 25, 2003.

2 *2.9%, 2.1 million*: Richard Willing, "Inmate Population Rises as Crime Drops," *USA Today*, July 28, 2003; *Probation and Parole in the United States, 2001* (Washington DC: Bureau of Justice Statistics, August 2002); Richard Willing, "US Prison Populations on the Rise," *USA Today*, May 28, 2004, p. 3A.

2 *25%, 83%, 136%*: Ken Stolle, "Virginia's Sentencing Guidelines Are a Model for the Nation," *Virginian-Pilot*, December 14, 2003, p. J1.

2 *$57 billion*: *Justice Expenditures and Employment in the United States* (Washington DC: Bureau of Justice Statistics, 1999), Table 3; Fox Butterfield, "With Longer Sentences, Cost of Fighting Crime Is Higher," *New York Times*, May 3, 2004.

2 *2.6%, 3.6%*: Willing, "Inmate Population," op. cit.

2 *30%, 1.2%, 18.2%*: Tara-Jen Ambrosio and Vincent Schiraldi, *From Classrooms to Cellblocks* (Washington DC: Justice Policy Institute, 1999).

2 *California built twenty-one*: *Cellblocks or Classrooms?* (Washington DC: Justice Policy Institute, 2002).

4 *$761 million, $615 million, fifty states*: Ibid.

4 *$10,000*: Salary figures for 1996; Daniel Burton Rose, ed.,

The Celling of America (Monroe, ME: Common Courage Press, 1998), p. 134.

4   *more state funds*: NYDOCS is ranked #1 in "general fund, state operations" spending; SUNY is a bigger agency, but only because it also receives federal offset funds; source: New York State Division of the Budget, personal communication to Sarah J. Gallogly, September 17, 2003.

4   *largest public sector employer, $1 billion, $400 million*: Frank Green, "Prison Chief Defends Tenure," *Richmond Times-Dispatch*, September 16, 2002, p. B1; Matthew Bowers, "Candidates Agree on Lack of Funding for Education," *Virginian-Pilot*, October 20, 2003, p. B1; Philip Walzer and Kristin King, "College Funding May Lack Attention," *Virginian-Pilot*, October 20, 2003, p. B6.

MYTH 1

PAGE

7   *100 per 100,000, 715 per 100,000*: Marc Mauer, *Race to Incarcerate* (New York: The New Press, 1999), pp. 82–84; Willing, "Inmate Population," op. cit.; Connie Cass, "Prison Population Grows by 2.9% in 2003," Associated Press, May 28, 2004.

7   *5.6 million, 11.3%*: Richard Willing, "More Adults Have Prison Experience," *USA Today*, August 18, 2003, p. 3A; see also Associated Press story, same date.

7   *1.5 million*: Neely Tucker, "Study Warns of Rising Tide of Released Inmates," *Washington Post*, May 21, 2003, p. A1.

8   *4.6%, 22%*: Roy Walmsley, *World Prison Population List*, 3rd ed. (London: Home Office Research, Development and Statistics Directorate, 2002); US Census Bureau, 2002.

8   *45 per 100,000, 143 per 100,000*: Walmsley, op. cit., pp. 4–5; Cass, "Prison," op. cit.

8   *21 to 24%*: Pat Mayhew and Jan J.M. Van Dijk, *Criminal Victimization in Eleven Industrialized Countries: Key Findings from the 1996 International Crime Victims Survey* (The Hague: Research and Documentation Centre, Ministry of Justice, 1997); J. Van Kesteren, P. Mayhew, P. Niewbeerta, *Criminal Victimization in Seventeen Industrialized Countries: Key Findings from the 2000 International Crime Victims*

Survey (The Hague: Research and Documentation Centre, Ministry of Justice, 2000).

8   *5.6, 2.4*: James Lynch, "Crime in International Perspective," in James Q. Wilson and Joan Petersilia, eds., *Crime* (San Francisco: Institute for Contemporary Studies, 1995), pp. 22–23.

9   *Canadian rates*: Carl T. Bogus, "The Strong Case for Gun Control," *American Prospect*, Summer 1992, pp. 19–28.

9   *"a group of English-speaking"*: Marc Mauer and Meda Chesney-Lind, eds., *Invisible Punishment: The Collateral Consequences of Mass Imprisonment* (New York: The New Press, 2003), p. 284.

9   *20%, "intelligent punishment"*: Caroline Schmidt, "Schwitzen Statt Sitzen," *Der Spiegel*, No. 30, 2003, p. 46.

11   *21.3%, 57.9%*: *Sourcebook of Criminal Justice Statistics 2000* (Washington DC: Bureau of Justice Statistics, 2000), Table 6.39.

12   *"deviant, delinquent"*: John J. DiIulio Jr., "The Question of Black Crime," *Public Interest*, Fall 1994, pp. 3–12.

12   *"After two decades"*: Cal Thomas, "Three Strikes and You're Broke," *Tribune Media Services*, November 17, 2003.

MYTH 2

PAGE

15   *"very large increases"*: Wilson and Petersilia, *Crime*, op. cit., p. 105.

15   *25%, 1%*: Christopher Nutall, "What Works in Dealing with Crime? An International Perspective," in *International Comparisons in Criminal Justice* (London: National Association for the Care and Resettlement for Offenders, 1995), p. 10.

15   *300%, marginally, hardly at all*: Franklin E. Zimring and Gordon Hawkins, *Incapacitation: Penal Confinement and the Restraint of Crime* (Oxford University Press, 1995). Less than 4 crimes annually were prevented by locking up one person for one year, and 3.25 of those were non-violent property offenses. Per prisoner-year, just 0.055 rapes and 0.007 homicides were prevented.

15   *"SPP changes have little"*: Thomas B. Marvell and Carlisle E.

Moody Jr., "Prison Population Growth and Crime Reduction," *Journal of Quantitative Criminology*, Vol. 10, No. 2, 1994, pp. 109–137.

15   *"does not appear to achieve"*: Jaqueline Cohen, *Incapacitating Criminals: Recent Research Findings* (Washington DC: National Institute of Justice, December 1983), pp. 3, 5.

16   *20%*: Etienne Benson, "Rehabilitate or Punish?," *Monitor on Psychology* (American Psychological Association), Vol. 34, No. 7, July–August 2003, p. 47.

16   *37%, 33%*: *Substance Abuse and Treatment, State and Federal Prisoners, 1997* (Washington DC: Bureau of Justice Statistics, 1997), p. 1.

16   *19%, 40%*: Education as Crime Prevention, OSI Criminal Justice Initiative, September 1997.

16   *8 to 10*: University of Cincinnati criminal justice professor Francis T. Cullen, in Warren St. John, "Professors With a Past," *New York Times*, August 9, 2003, p. A13.

16   *38%*: Mauer, *Race*, op. cit., p. 110.

17   *peak ages*: Ibid., p. 112.

18   *625,000*: Tucker, "Study," op. cit.

18   *67.5%, 51.8%, 165,000, 158,750*: Patrick A. Langan and David J. Levin, *Recidivism of Prisoners Released in 1994* (Washington DC: Bureau of Justice Statistics, June 2002).

18   *300,000*: Tucker, "Study," op. cit.

19   *3,932,751*: *Probation and Parole*, op. cit.

19   *14%*: Richard Willing, "Jail Populations Strain Cash-Strapped Communities," *USA Today*, August 21, 2003, p. 2A.

19   *2.6%*: Willing, "Inmate Population," op. cit.

19   *"I think every"*: Frank Green, "More Prisons for Va.—But How Many?," *Richmond Times-Dispatch*, March 1, 2004, p. A1.

19   *one third, "failed drug tests"*: Calculation based on VDOC data in Louis Hansen, "Va. Prisons Tight, Getting Tighter," *Virginian-Pilot*, February 15, 2004.

21   *In Virginia, 46%*: Ibid.

21   *"No one is more"*: Joan Petersilia, *When Prisoners Come Home* (New York: Oxford University Press, 2003).

22   *"The American incarceration rate"*: Public Education Speaker Kit, Module 5, "Incarceration," Correctional Service of Canada, www. csc-scc.gc/ca.

22   *"among mainstream politicians"*: Mauer, *Invisible*, op. cit., p. 280.

MYTH 3

PAGE

24   more *likely*: James Q. Finckenhauer and Patricia W. Gavin, *Scared Straight: The Panacea Phenomenon Revisited* (Prospect Heights, IL: Waveland Press, 1999).

24   *Project DARE*: Fox Butterfield, no headline, *New York Times* News Service online, April 16, 1997, 7:06 E.S.T., citing Office of Justice Programs, *Preventing Crime: What Works, What Doesn't, What's Promising* (Washington DC: U.S. Department of Justice, 1997).

25   *"effective in reducing"*: Steven Schlossman et al., *Delinquency Prevention in Southern Chicago: A Fifty-Year Assessment of the Chicago Area Project* (Santa Monica, CA: RAND Corp., 1984).

25   *Twenty-seven years, one-fifth, one-fourth*: Lawrence Schweinhart, H.V. Barnes, David Weikart, *Significant Benefits: The High/Scope Perry Preschool Study Through Age 27* (Ypsilanti, MI: High/Scope Press, 1993); Deanna S. Gomby et al., "Long-term Outcomes of Early Childhood Programs," *The Future of Children*, Vol. 5, No. 3, Winter 1995.

25   *Syracuse University*: Elliott Currie, *Crime and Punishment in America* (New York: Henry Holt & Co., 1998), p. 97.

26   *46%, 27%, one third, half*: Tim Stafford, "The Criminologists Who Discovered Churches," *Christianity Today*, June 14, 1999.

26   *"concluded rather convincingly"*: John Braithwaite, "The Myth of Social Class and Criminality Reconsidered," *American Sociological Review*, Vol. 46, No. 1, 1981, pp. 36–57; see also studies by D.S. Elliott, N.H. Rafter, M. Farnworth.

26   *study of AFDC*: James DeFronzo, "AFDC, a City's Racial and Ethnic Composition, and Burglary," *Social Service Review*, September 1996, pp. 464–471; James DeFronzo, "Welfare and Homicide," *Journal of Research in Crime and Delinquency*, Vol. 34, No. 3, August 1997.

26   *international comparisons*: "Measuring the Impact of Imprisonment: Papers from a Roundtable Held in London on

9 November 2001" (London, England: International Centre for Prison Studies, July 2002), p. 28.

28   *$14,480*: Associated Press, "Census Survey: More in Poverty," *Richmond Times-Dispatch*, September 3, 2003, p. A13.

28   *3.8 million, 11 million*: Associated Press, "Report Says US Hunger Level Is Rising," *Virginian-Pilot*, November 3, 2003, p. A6.

28   *$55.18*: 1996 cost; *Statistical Abstract of the United States 2001: The National Data Book* (Austin, TX: Hoover's, Inc., 2002), Table 333.

28   *36%*: Charles W. Colson, *Justice That Restores* (Wheaton, IL: Tyndale House Publishers, 2001), p. 201.

29   *associated with fatherless*: Kevin N. Wright and Karen E. Wright, *Family Life, Delinquency, and Crime: A Policymaker's Guide* (Washington DC: US Department of Justice, 1995).

29   *six times*: Barbara D. Whitehead, "Dan Quayle Was Right," *Atlantic Monthly*, Vol. 271, No. 4, April 1993, p. 47.

29   *60%, 72%, 70%*: Colson, *Justice*, op. cit., p. 101.

29   *PEIP in Elmira*: Currie, *Crime*, op. cit., p. 83.

29   *RAND Corporation study*: Peter Greenwood, *The Cost-Effectiveness of Early Intervention as a Strategy for Reducing Violent Crime* (Santa Monica, CA: RAND Corp., 1995), p. 20.

30   *"a second chance"*: *Achieving Justice and Reversing the Problem of Gang Crime and Gang Violence in America Today* (Chicago: National Gang Crime Research Center, 1996).

30   *three times, twice as likely*: Carolyn Smith and Terence P. Thornberry, "The Relationship Between Childhood Maltreatment and Adolescent Involvement in Delinquency," *Criminology*, Vol. 33, No. 4, 1995, pp. 451–477; see also Cathy Spatz Widom, *The Cycle of Violence Revisited* (Washington DC: National Institute of Justice, 1996).

30   *38%*: Frank Schmalleger, *Criminology Today: An Integrative Introduction*, 2nd ed. (Upper Saddle River, NJ: Prentice-Hall Inc., 1999, 1996), p. 27.

30   *16.1%, 57.2%*: Caroline W. Harlow, "Prior Abuse Reported by Inmates and Probationers," *Bureau of Justice Selected Findings* (Washington DC: US Department of Justice, 1999).

31   *1.5 million*: Tucker, "Study," op. cit.

31   *17.2%, 12.2 million*: Associated Press, "Census Survey," op. cit.

31   *twenty-eight states failed*: Laura Meckler, Associated Press, "States Fail Rigorous Child-Protection Test," *Richmond Times-Dispatch*, August 19, 2003.

31   *one million substantiated cases*: John J. DiIulio Jr., "Two Million Prisoners Are Enough," *Wall Street Journal*, March 12, 1999.

32   *"A growing prison"*: Currie, *Crime*, op. cit., p. 32.

32   *"the internationally recognized"*: Mauer, *Invisible*, op. cit., p. 281.

32   *4%, 6%, 22%*: Lee Rainwater and Timothy M. Smeeding, *Doing Poorly: The Real Income of American Children in a Comparative Perspective* (Syracuse University: Maxwell School of Citizenship and Public Affairs, 1995).

MYTH 4

PAGE

34   *6%*: Ayelish McGarvey, "Reform Done Right," *American Prospect*, December 2003, p. 43.

34   *40%, 17%*: *The Health Status of Soon-to-Be-Released Inmates: A Report to Congress* (Washington DC: National Commission on Correctional Care, November–December 2002), p. xii.

34   *three psychiatrists, 8,000, two days*: Fox Butterfield, "Study Finds Hundreds of Thousands of Inmates Mentally Ill," *New York Times*, October 22, 2003.

34   *a recent study, 25%*: Paul von Zielbauer, "Report on State Prisons Cites Inmates' Mental Illness," *New York Times*, October 22, 2003.

34   *14%, 18%*: *Substance Abuse*, op. cit., p.1.

34   *23.4%*: *Education and Correctional Population* (Washington DC: Bureau of Justice Statistics, January 2003), Table 4.

34   *half of America's, 90%*: Jessica Partner, "Jailed Youths Shortchanged on Education," *Education Week*, Vol. XVI, No. 5, October 2, 1996.

35   *$35,000, $5,000, $7,300, $21,000, $29,800*: Ronald Fraser, DKT Liberty Project.

35   *4%*: *Ready, Willing and Able: What the Record Shows About*

State Investment in Children, 1990–1995 (Washington DC: National Association of Child Advocates, 1996), p. 46.

35 *Twenty years ago*: Jens Soering, *The Way of the Prisoner: Breaking the Chains of Self Through Centering Prayer and Centering Practice* (New York: Lantern Books, 2003).

36 *350, 12, elimination of Pell Grants*: www.changingminds.ws/ brochure, viewed January 3, 2003.

36 *"Education yourself"*: *Anger Management Program Participant's Manual* (Richmond, VA: Virginia Department of Corrections, no date), Handout 3–1.

36 *25.9%*: *Follow-up Study of a Sample of Offenders Who Earned High School Equivalency Diplomas (GED) While Incarcerated in DOCS* (New York Department of Correctional Services, May 2001), Figure 1.

36 *half the rate*: *Analysis of Return Dates of the Inmate College Program Participants* (New York Department of Correctional Services, August 1991).

38 *$46.2 million, cut in half, eliminated*: State of California, Governor's Budget Summary, 2003–04, p. 146; Samantha M. Shapiro, "Jails for Jesus," *Mother Jones*, November–December 2003, p. 57.

39 *"Treatment works"*: Vincent Schiraldi, "Prison Nation," *Virginian-Pilot*, December 14, 2003, p. J1

39 *17.3%, 9.9%*: Karen Kersting, "New Hope for Sex Offender Treatment," *Monitor on Psychology* (American Psychological Association), Vol. 34, No. 7, July–August 2003, pp. 52–53, citing R. Karl Hanson's study in *Sex Abuse: A Journal of Research and Treatment*, Vol. 14, No. 2, 2002.

39 *"attitudes that led to offending"*: Researcher and law professor John Q. LaFond, J.D., University of Missouri–Kansas City, in Kersting, "New Hope," op. cit.

39 *not a single SORT*: Interview with SORT staff member who asked to remain anonymous, conducted by author on October 29, 2003.

40 *In the 1970s; "InnerChange Freedom Initiative"*: Colson, *Justice*, op. cit., p. 97.

40 *14%, 41%*: National Institute for Healthcare Research, "Religious Programs, Institutional Adjustment, and Recidivism Among Former Inmates in Prison Fellowship Programs," *Justice Quarterly*, Vol. 14, No. 1, March 1997, pp. 145–66.

40   *controversy about the effectiveness*: Shapiro, "Jails," op. cit., p. 98.

41   *Restorative Prison Project, 90%, "change any negative"*: Jennifer Dinsdale, "Restorative Justice in H.M. Prison Holme House" (London, England: International Centre for Prison Studies, 2001), p. 54.

41   *"restorative justice counselor"*: Mauer, *Invisible*, op. cit., p. 285.

41   *"cooperat[ion] with local partner"*: Dutch Correctional Services, www. dji.nl.

42   *Act of 1996*: Mauer, *Invisible*, op. cit., pp. 18, 44.

42   *Act of 1998*: Tucker, "Study," op. cit.

42   *"All the things"*: Tucker, "Study," op. cit.

43   *2.28%*: Ugger and Mazza, "Democratic Contraction? Political Consequences of Felon Disenfranchisement in the US," *American Sociological Review*, Vol. 67, December 2002, Table A.

43   *great majority*: Mauer, *Invisible*, op. cit., p. 57.

44   *827,000, 31.2%*: Ugger and Mazza, "Contraction," op. cit., p. 798; Jamie Fellner and Marc Mauer, "Losing the Vote: The Impact of Felony Disenfranchisement in the US," The Sentencing Project and Human Rights Watch, October 1998, p. 9.

44   *"250,000 to 600,000"*: Michael M. Horrock, "Hundreds of Thousands Raped in US Lockups," United Press International, July 31, 2002.

44   *8.5%*: *HIV in Prisons* (Washington DC: Bureau of Justice Statistics, 2000), p. 2.

44   *0.3%*: Centers for Disease Control, "Morbidity and Mortality Weekly Report," February 26, 2003, Vol. 52.

44   *14,500*: *Profile of State Prisoners Under Age 18, 1985–1997* (Washington DC: Bureau of Justice Statistics, February 2000), pp. 1, 2.

MYTH 5

PAGE

48   *42% to 20%, $23,800, $668, $4,187*: Kathryn Bridges, "Changes at Probation and Parole Save Money," *Daily Herald* (North Carolina), July 16, 2003, p. A1.

48   *7.5, 16%, 27%*: Florida Department of Corrections, Bureau

of Research and Data Analysis, "Community Control/Electronic Monitoring Admissions from July 1, 1993, to June 30, 1999—Outcomes of June 30, 1999"; Colson, *Justice*, op. cit. p. 134.

50 *30,468, 160,000, "at some point"*: Patrick McMahon, "States Cut Inmates Loose to Cut Costs," *USA Today*, August 11, 2003, p. 1A.

51 *$250 million*: Drake Bennett and Robert Kuttner, "Crime and Redemption," *American Prospect*, December 2003.

51 *every dollar spent, seven dollars*: *Evaluating Recovery Services: The California Drug and Alcohol Treatment Assessment* (Sacramento, CA: State of California Department of Alcohol and Drug Programs, April 1994), p. 89.

51 *RAND Corporation*: Jonathan P. Caulkins et al., *Mandatory Minimum Drug Sentences: Throwing Away the Key or the Taxpayers' Money?* (Santa Monica, CA: RAND Corp., 1997).

51 *poll of police chiefs*: *Drugs and Crime Across America— Police Chiefs Speak Out: A National Survey Among Chiefs of Police Conducted for Police Foundation and Drug Strategies* (Washington DC: Peter D. Hart Research Associates, 1996).

51 *"RELEASE drug-only offenders"*: DiIulio, "Two Million," op. cit.

52 *ABC News poll*: "Treatment Over Jail Time," ABC News, abcnews.go.com, June 13, 2001.

53 *"prisons have really become"*: Benson, "Rehabilitate," op. cit., p. 47.

53 *80,000*: Butterfield, "Study," op. cit.

54 *"enormous, unusual agreement"*: Jamie Fellner, director of the United States program at Human Rights Watch, in Butterfield, "Study," op. cit.

55 *77 to 85%*: Deborah Smith Bailey, "Alternatives to Incarceration," *Monitor on Psychology* (American Psychological Association), Vol. 34, No. 7, July–August 2003, pp. 56, 55.

55 *McNaughten Rule*: Schmalleger, *Criminology*, op. cit., pp. 252–256.

56 *Ricky Ray Rector*: Mauer, *Race*, p. 69.

56 *recent studies*: Beth Edmonson, "Teenage Sniper Suspect Shouldn't Be Tried as Adult," *Virginian-Pilot*, November 10, 2003, p. B11.

57 *court-ordered child murders*: "Malvo Likely Won't Be Part of

Campaign to End Juvenile Death Penalty," CNN.com, January 7, 2003.

57   *Washington State Institute*: Tori DeAngelis, "Youth Programs Cut Crime, Costs," *Monitor on Psychology* (American Psychological Association), Vol. 34, No. 7, July–August 2003, pp. 48–49; see also www.colorado.edu/cspv/blueprints.

57   *"We've come a long way"*: Sam V. Meddis and Patricia Edmonds, "Rehabilitation on a Small Scale," *USA Today*, September 29, 1994, p. 10A.

58   *27,000*: Frank Green, "Technical Violations Mount," *Richmond Times-Dispatch*, January 21, 2003, p. B1.

59   *"in the 1990s"*: Henry Ruth and Keith R. Reitz, *The Challenge of Crime: Rethinking Our Response* (Harvard University Press, 2003), pp. 95–96.

59   *rates similar, much shorter*: Warren Young and Mark Brown, "Cross-National Comparisons of Imprisonment," in Michael Tonry, ed., *Crime and Justice: A Review of Research*, Vol. 17 (Chicago: University of Chicago Press, 1994), pp. 1–49.

59   *Canadian burglar*: James Lynch, "Crime in International Perspective," in Wilson and Petersilia, *Crime*, op. cit., pp. 11–38.

59   *British robber*: David Farrington and Patrick A. Langan, "Changes in Crime and Punishment in England and America in the 1980s," *Justice Quarterly*, Vol. 9, No. 1, March 1992, pp. 5–18.

59   *approaches zero, less than a quarter*: Mauer, *Race*, op. cit., p. 112.

59   *"Most men age"*: "Can Parole Cut Crime?," *Parade*, December 10, 2003, p. 17.

59   *41%*: Allen Beck and Bernard Shipley, *Recidivism of Prisoners Released in 1983* (Washington DC: Bureau of Justice Statistics, April 1989).

60   *1.4%*: *Probation and Parole Violators in State Prisons, 1991* (Washington DC: Bureau of Justice Statistics, August, 1995).

60   *125,000, one third*: Stefanie Pfeiffer, "One Strike Against the Elderly: Growing Old in Prison," Medill News Service, August 2002; US Census Bureau, quoted in Joshua Maher, "The Quality of Care of Elderly Inmates in Prison," KELN.org, May 2000. Penologists define "elderly" as fifty-five and over for convicts; prisoners' physical age is generally ten years higher than their chronological age due to poor health.

60 *three times, $5 billion*: Jim Krane, "The Graying of America's Prisons: An Emerging Corrections Crisis," APB News, April 12, 1999; Matthew Nehmer, "GW Professor Jonathan Turley to Testify," GW News Center, George Washington University, February 24, 2003.

60 *"inmates in wheelchairs"*: Jennifer Warren, "The Graying of the Prisons," *Los Angeles Times*, June 9, 2002.

62 *Supreme Court ruled*: Lockyer v. Andrade, 123 S.Ct. 1166 (2003); see also Ewing v. California, 123 S.Ct. 1179 (2003).

64 *"We assume that"*: Frank Green, "Parole Policy Unused," *Richmond Times-Dispatch*, September 14, 2003, p. B1.

64 *127,677, Sentencing Project*: Donna Leinwand, "Study Cites Sentencing Laws for Rise in Prison Life Terms," *USA Today*, May 12, 2004.

64 *15.6%, five of these lifers*: John E. Dannenberg, "Bloated Prison Budget Fuels California's Degenerative Incarceration Spiral," *Prison Legal News*, November 2003, p. 2, based on reports in the *Los Angeles Times, San Francisco Chronicle, Sacramento Bee, AlterNet, Fresno Bee*, and *Oakland Tribune*.

65 *lowest recidivism rate*: Langan and Levin, *Recidivism*, op. cit.

65 *POPS Program*: www.gwu.edu/~ccommit/law.htm, "POPS Program Gives a Second Chance," May 26, 2003.

65 *TOP Program*: Colson, *Justice*, op. cit., p. 137.

65 *Charles "Joe" Hynes*: Bruce Western, "Lawful Re-Entry," *American Prospect*, December 2003, p. 55.

66 *Chicago's Safer Foundation*: McGarvey, "Reform," op. cit.

66 *Delancey Street Restaurant*: Adam Cohen, "A Community of Ex-Cons Shows How to Bring Prisoners Back Into Society," *New York Times*, January 2, 2004.

66 *Crossover Restorative Ministries*: Braxton Williams, "Crossover Rebuilds People's Potential," *Richmond Times-Dispatch*, January 24, 2004.

66 *VJO Program*: Jeffrey Fagan, "Treatment and Reintegration of Violent Juvenile Offenders: Experimental Results," *Justice Quarterly*, Vol. 7, 1990, pp. 233–363; Jeffrey Fagan and Martin Frost, "Risks, Fixes and Zeal: Implementing Experimental Treatments for Violent Juvenile Offenders," *The Prison Journal*, Vol. 67, No. 1, March 1996, pp. 22–59.

67 *only for non-violent*: Virginia Department of Corrections memorandum on Offender Re-Entry Program, displayed on prison bulletin boards and viewed by author on March 3, 2004.

67   *"Forgiveness is not just"*: Charles M. Sennott, "Pilgrimage of Forgiveness," *America*, November 10, 2003, p. 9.

67   *"emphatic . . . rejection"*: Mauer, *Invisible*, op. cit., p. 281.

68   *"Our resources are misspent"*: CBS Evening News, August 10, 2003.

MYTH 6

PAGE

71   *"loss of quality of life"*: Ted R. Miller, Mark A. Cohen, and Brian Wiersma, *Victim Costs and Consequences: A New Look* (Washington DC: National Institute of Justice, 1996).

71   *$345 billion*: Currie, *Crime*, op. cit., p. 72.

71   *Zedlewski's methodology*: Mauer, *Race*, op. cit., pp. 64–66.

72   *3,700*: Currie, *Crime*, op. cit., p. 68.

72   *largest contributor, $2 million*: Pamela McLean, "Strong Arm of the Law," *San Francisco Bay Guardian*, December 4, 2002.

72   *$251,000, 34%*: "Prison Guards' Sick Leave Usage Soars as Rules Shift," *Los Angeles Times*, June 27, 2002.

72   *half a million*: Christian Parenti, *Lockdown America* (New York: Verso Press, 2000).

72   *"implementing a policy," "aggravating tensions," "the governor does not"*: Laura Mansuerus, "Prison Union Seeks Ouster of the Chief of Corrections," *New York Times*, December 31, 2003.

73   *"While arrest rates and convictions"*: Jennifer L. Beck, World Research Group, conference invitation letter, December 1996.

73   *41%, 15%, 190%*: James Austin and Garry Coventry, "Are We Better Off? Comparing Private and Public Prisons in the United States," *Current Issues in Criminal Justice*, Vol. 2, No. 2, 1999; Oklahoma Department of Corrections figures, presented by Dennis Cunningham at the World Research Group conference, "Privatizing Correctional Facilities," September 25, 2000, in San Antonio, TX.

73   *142, 521, $2 billion*: Private Adult Correctional Facility Census, 1996 and 2001 editions, quoted in Peter Wagner, *The Prison Index* (Springfield, MA: Prison Policy Initiative, 2003), p. 36.

73   *$58 million, $2.32, "inexcusable," "near riot"*: "State: Prison Food Costs Less, but at a Price," *St. Petersburg Times*, June 17, 2002.

75   *$15,000, $3,000*: Joel Dyer, *The Perpetual Prisoner Machine* (Boulder, CO: Westview Press, 2000), p. 14.

75   *60%, $6 to $8 million, declared illegal, third-largest contribution*: Bill Sizemore, "Prison Calls Prove Boon for Virginia," *Virginian-Pilot*, February 1, 2004, p. A1.

76   *"infested with spiders," twice the national average, "provides quality, compassionate"*: Adam Liptak, "Alabama Prison at Center of Suit Over AIDS Policy," *New York Times*, October 26, 2003.

76   *"there was never any"*: Karen Olsson, "Ghostwriting the Law," MotherJones.com, September–October 2002.

77   *six correctional facilities, 5,094, 1,584*: Francis X. Donnelly, "Ionia Finds Stability in Prisons," *Detroit News*, July 15, 2001.

77   *60%*: Calvin L. Beale, "Rural Prisons: An Update," *Rural Development Perspectives*, Vol. 2, No. 2, p. 25.

77   *Urban Institute*: Fox Butterfield, "Study Tracks Boom in Prisons and Notes Impact on Counties," *New York Times*, April 30, 2004.

77   *residents* in their prisons: Peter Wagner, "Prisoner Disenfranchisement and State Legislative Redistricting in New York State," unpublished ms., November 2001, cited in Wagner, *Index*, p. 38.

77   *6.99%*: Peter Wagner, "Importing Constituents: Prisoners and Political Clout in New York" (Springfield, MA: Prison Policy Initiative, 2002), p. 8.

77   *fastest growing, 23%*: Tracy Huling, "Prisoners of the Census," MoJo Wire, *Mother Jones*, May 10, 2000.

78   *$5 and $8 million*: "Detaining for dollars," Prison Policy Initiative fact sheet, September 4, 2002.

78   *8.8 million, 4.8 million, 1.4 million*: Bekah Wright, Four14 Communications, "Telling You What You Already 'Feel' in the Job Market," *Richmond Times-Dispatch*, April 14, 2003.

79   *about two thirds*: Elliott Currie, *Crime*, op. cit.

79   *tuberculosis in New York*: Laurie Garrett, *The Coming Plague: Newly Emerging Diseases in a World Out of Balance* (New York: Farrar, Straus & Giroux, 1994), pp. 523–34.

79   *2.2%, 0.8%, 2%*: Frank Green, "US, Virginia Inmate AIDS Cases Down," *Richmond Times-Dispatch*, September 2, 2003, p. A8.

79   *0.3%*: Centers for Disease Control, "Morbidity and Mortality Weekly Report," February 26, 2003, Vol. 52.

80   *8.5%*: *HIV in Prisons*, op. cit., p. 2.

80   *twenty states*: Liptak, "Alabama Prisons," op. cit.

80   *have to see the doctor*: Response to author's "Informal Mechanism" by Brunswick Correctional Center Medical Department staff member, October 27, 2003.

80   *"Recommendations and Reports"*: Centers for Disease Control, "Recommendations and Reports," MMWR 2003, Vol. 52, No. RR-1, January 24, 2003.

80   *16 and 41%, $15,000 to $25,000, "only fifty inmates"*: Michael Hardy, "ACLU: Prison Care Lacking," *Richmond Times-Dispatch*, May 8, 2003, p. A1.

80   *"Correctional systems have"*: Quoted in Mark Wilson, "America's Prisons Turn a Blind Eye to HCV Epidemic," *Prison Legal News*, Vol. 14, No. 8, p. 1.

81   *5.1%, 71%*: *Sourcebook 2000*, op. cit., Table 2.36, calculation based on Table 4.2.

81   *336%, 13%*: "Network News in the Nineties," *Media Monitor*, July–August 1997, p. 2.

81   *Lawrence Grossman*: Lawrence K. Grossman, "Why Local TV News Is So Awful," *Columbia Journalism Review*, November–December 1997, p. 21.

81   *"Predators get amenities"*: Juan Antonio Lizama, "Predators Get Amenities," *Richmond Times-Dispatch*, September 17, 2003.

82   *"Hound him"*: Ron French, "Convicted Sexual Predator Finds No Post-Prison Solace," *Detroit News*, July 27, 2003, p. A1.

CONCLUSION

PAGE

85   *990, 6,838*: *Sourcebook 2000*, op. cit., Table 6.10.

85   *851*: Marc Mauer, "Americans Behind Bars: The International Use of Incarceration, 1992–1993," cited in Wagner, *Index*, op. cit., p. 41.

85   *More than one fifth*: Tucker, "Study," op. cit.

85   *half of all young*: Eric Lottke, *Hobbling a Generation* (Baltimore: National Center on Institutions and Alternatives, 1997); see also *Washington Post*, August 26, 1997, p. B1.

86   *21%, 50%*: Mauer, *Race*, op. cit.

86   *twenty-five states*: Fox Butterfield, "With Cash Tight, States

Reassess Long Jail Terms," *New York Times*, November 10, 2003.

86   *Milliken, Dunne, Allen*: Schiraldi, "Prison Nation," op. cit.; Bennett and Kuttner, "Crime and Redemption," op. cit., p. 36.

87   *4%, 6%*: Vincent Schiraldi, "California's Prison System Lags Behind," Pacific News Service, June 30, 2003.

87   *"gravely concerned," likely to be terminated*: John M. Broder, "Dismal California Prisons Hold Juvenile Offenders," *New York Times*, February 15, 2004.

88   *Ehrlich, "to get non-violent drug"*: Schiraldi, "Prison Nation," op. cit.

88   *7.2 million, 30 million, 30%*: Schiraldi, "Prison Nation," op. cit.; Louis Hansen, "Va. Prisons," op. cit., p. A1.

88   *John Ashcroft*: *New York Times* News Service, "Rehnquist Considers New Law an Affront," *Richmond Times-Dispatch*, January 2, 2004.

89   *60%*: *Sourcebook 2000*, op. cit., Table 6.51; UNICOR Annual Report 2001, p. 13.

89   *"fiscal pressures may"*: Alan Elsner, "America's Prison Habit," *Washington Post*, January 24, 2004.

89   *"public interest" proposal*: I proposed this plan initially in "Smells Like Change," published by *Fortune News*, XXXIV, No. 4, p. 10.

90   *"some prisons have actually"*: "The Dark Side of America," *New York Times*, May 17, 2004.

90   *faith-based proposal*: I proposed this plan initially in "The Perils of Freedom," *America* magazine, July 5–12, 2004.

91   *134, 317,580*: William A. McGeveran Jr., ed., *The World Almanac and Book of Facts 2001* (Mahwah, NJ: World Almanac Education Group, 2001), pp. 689–690; calculation excludes Seventh Day Adventist, Christian Scientist, Jehovah's Witness, Latter-Day Saints, and all non-Christian faiths.

INDEX

About the Author

Jens Soering has been incarcerated since 1986. His case has been featured on Court TV, Discovery Channel, and A&E. He is the author of *The Way of the Prisoner: Breaking the Chains of Self Through Centering Prayer and Centering Practice* (Lantern Books, 2003), and has written for newspapers in Virginia, Pennsylvania, and Washington DC, as well as for *America, National Catholic Reporter, Sojourners*, and many other publications.

See www.jenssoering.com.